INVESTING
IN VICE

INVESTING
IN VICE

The Recession-Proof Portfolio
of Booze, Bets, Bombs, and Butts

DAN AHRENS

ST. MARTIN'S PRESS ▩▩ NEW YORK

This book is for informational purposes only and is not intended to provide personalized investment advice. The investment approaches described in this book may not be appropriate for any particular investor's needs, financial situation, and investment objectives. In addition, investors are advised that past stock performance is no guarantee of future price appreciation.

Library of Congress Cataloging-in-Publication Data

Ahrens, Dan.
    Investing in vice : the recession-proof portfolio of booze, bets, bombs, and butts / Dan Ahrens.
        p. cm.
    Includes index (page 137).
    ISBN 0-312-32504-5
    1. Investments—Moral and ethical aspects.   I. Title.

HG4515.13.A47 2004
332.63'22—dc22

2003058638

First Edition: February 2004

10 9 8 7 6 5 4 3 2 1

Contents

A Note to Readers

The opinions expressed in this book are those of the author alone, not the publisher, and not necessarily those of MUTUALS.com, Inc., MUTUALS Holding Corp., or the MUTUALS.com Vice Fund. Moreover, opinions are subject to change, are not guaranteed, and should not be considered a recommendation to buy or sell any individual security. In particular, there are risks involved in investing in industries that may be adversely affected by legislative initiatives as well as changes in economic conditions, all of which may impact profitability in those industries.

Acknowledgments

This book, and my "vice" portfolio itself, wouldn't have been possible without the contributions of a myriad of people. I'd like to thank my wonderful wife, Jane Ahrens, who helps keep me balanced with her contributions to charitable causes, her incessant recycling, and her great work with sustainable (green) architecture. Charles Salzberg, a great writer and teacher of writing, has helped me immensely. My agent, Paul Fedorko, and George Witte of St. Martin's Press handled this book from its conception. I'd like to thank Marie Estrada at St. Martin's and attorney Josh Rubins. I'd also like to thank everyone at MUTUALS.com, especially CEO Rick Sapio, Brian Bull, Michael Henry, Michele Leftwich, and Brian Scheibmeir for their constant hard work and dedication; and fund co-manager Eric McDonald for adding a number of his opinions and ideas to the book.

Acknowledgments

Our fund administrators and distributors are at U.S. Bancorp Fund Services and Quasar Distributors, LLC. The people there include Katie Barry, Josie Hollman, Bea Spoerl, Jim Tiegs, Elaine Richards, Chad Fickett, Bob Kern, Joe Neuberger, Joe Redwine, Jim Schoenike, Teresa Cowan, Suzanne Riley, Naiomi Lundman, Susan Bishop, and Michele Adyniec. Also, Amy Stewart, of Stewart Design in Dallas, did a great Web site and logo design.

Thank you to all the people who have "invested in vice" and stuck with it, especially those who made great comments to the press like Dr. Lorin Berland, Bruce McClure, and Shalmir Tippit.

And to the many people with whom I've shared a drink, a good cigar, or a friendly (or not so friendly) game of poker, cheers.

INVESTING IN VICE

Introduction

Vices are not crimes.

—Lysander Spooner, legal writer, 1875

The goal of investing money is to make a profit.

Unfortunately, reaching that goal isn't always easy, especially in turbulent economic times.

Through the 1990s and into the twenty-first century, the bulls were loose in the street, as Americans invested at an unprecedented rate. The mutual fund industry grew from fewer than 2,500 available funds to more than 10,000. Online trading exploded onto the scene, as millions of Americans spent hours in front of their computers tracking stock prices, waiting to pounce on the latest IPOs, and gathering often dubious information from chat rooms. Old-style pensions became dinosaurs, and the 401(k) market boomed. Ordinary people, some of whom had never invested in the stock market before, were choosing their own investments, suddenly thinking of themselves as investment experts.

Business news became front-page news and, as a result of the unprecedented media hype, which was then often passed on at the office water cooler, investors were bombarded with what passed as sage advice like, "Invest now, or you'll miss the boat," and "Do it yourself, don't pay a professional." And that's exactly what we did, as we giddily invested our money in the tech boom, where stock prices became so inflated that it was not unusual to see a company's stock price rise 20, 30, or even 40 percent in a day. Of course, that couldn't last and it didn't. By the spring of 2000, the bubble burst and stock prices tumbled precipitously as investors lost millions of dollars in the market, and Internet stocks, which had been trading at over a hundred dollars a share, suddenly were worth less than the price of a candy bar.

The past three years have turned out to be one of the most difficult periods for investing, as the volatile Dow Jones Industrial Average seesawed up and down by as much as 300 or 400 points in a single day. Investors just couldn't get a handle on where to put their money.

Unfortunately, most small investors haven't listen closely to experienced and accomplished investors like Warren Buffett and Peter Lynch who have always preached, "Invest in what you know" and "Invest in what you understand." Many investors confused owning a computer with really knowing and understanding the semiconductor industry, or sending an E-mail with being an Internet industry authority.

After the market peak, we found ourselves in the midst of a recession which, no matter how much the Federal Reserve Board reduced interest rates in an effort to pump up the faltering economy, we couldn't quite seem to shake. Then came 9/11, which further shook consumer and investor confidence. And, as if that wasn't enough, accounting scandals involving major corporations like Enron and WorldCom eroded what little confidence Americans had in big business.

And yet, all this notwithstanding, the American economy is resilient and, despite bad economic times, Americans still need (and want) to invest their money. Simply putting it in banks or money markets, which yield less than 2 percent, is not enough.

During the poor stock market performance over the past few years, certain investment types and industries have performed comparatively well. They've risen to the top in part because the overall market has been in a funk. The price of gold, for instance, which had been mired in a slump for years, suddenly went through the roof. Other investment areas also showed top performance over a three-, five-, or ten-year period because they continued to perform respectably while the overall market dropped. Although the overall market seemed to fall off a cliff, some industries suddenly appeared as nearly "recession proof."

As it happens, among the areas that appeared to be recession proof were those industries that have been screened out by many investors and especially many of the so-called socially responsible investors as being "evil": alcohol, tobacco, gaming, and defense.

Is investing in vice or sin stocks a sound or legitimate idea? Based on the number of news stories in the media examining the subject, I certainly think so. I've only tracked stories on the subject since mid-2002, but the list is long. Here's a sampling of the coverage so you can research for yourself.

CNN
Jack Cafferty, *In the Money, Mutual Fund Makes Virtue Out of Vice,* June 22, 2003

Investing in Vice

CNBC-TV
Bertha Coombs, *How to Profit by Investing in Vice,* June 20, 2003

Dow Jones News Service
Tom Becker, *Tip Sheet: Mutuals.com Sees Investing Virtue in Vices,* June 13, 2003

Forbes.com
Christopher Helman, *Betting on the Vice Squad,* June 11, 2003

CNNfn
Pat Kiernan and Ali Velshi, *The Money Gang, Mutual Fundamentals: Making Money Off of Sin,* May 16, 2003

CNBC.com
Michael Brush, *Company Focus: Should You Abstain from Sin Stocks?,* April 23, 2003

***National Post* (Canada)**
Pierre Lemieux, *Does Vice Pay?,* April 4, 2003

Penthouse
Marianne Mancusi, *Sin Stocks,* April 2003

Value Line Insight
Jason Smith, *A Sinful Delight: Cashing In on Vice!,* March 2003

New Orleans Times-Picayune
Teresa Dixon Murray, *Vice Is Mutual Fund's Focus,* March 16, 2003

Introduction

Physicians Financial News
James Armstrong, *Investors Take a Gamble on Gaming Company Shares,* March 15, 2003

Toronto Star
Madhavi Acharya and Tom Yew, *Vice Takes Place Beside Virtue in Battle to Attract Investment,* March 3, 2003

National Post (Canada)
Susan Heinrich, *Selling a Mix of Profits and "Sin,"* February 20, 2003

CNN/Money.com
Paul R. La Monica, *Stocks for Homer Simpson,* February 6, 2003

CNNfn
Kathleen Hays, *Money and Markets: War and Investing,* February 5, 2003

Buyside Magazine
Meghan Leerskov, *Vice Is Nice: The Underbelly of the Investment World Isn't Such a Bad Place to Be,* January/ February 2003

The Star-Ledger (Newark, N.J.)
Fund Up Close: Vice Fund, January 23, 2003

Christianity Today
Ted Olsen, *Sin Sells,* January 21, 2003

Entrepreneur Magazine
Dian Vujovich, *Funds and Games: This Investment Is So Bad It Might Be Good,* January 2003

Investing in Vice

CNN Asia
Andrew Brown, *Vice Is Nice: Investors Cash In on Sin,* December 30, 2002

CNN International
Maggie Lake, *"Sin" Stocks: Recession Proof?,* December 13, 2002

CBS MarketWatch
William Spain, *Screens Are Keen but Liquor Is Quicker,* December 10, 2002

Atlanta Journal-Constitution
Bob Smietana, *A Penchant for "Sin": Mutual Fund Bets that Vice Is a Good Investment,* December 7, 2002

ABC News, Cleveland NewsChannel5
Adam Shapiro, *Investors Buying Stock in Sin,* November 26, 2002

New York Observer
Paul Sullivan, *Running with the Devil,* November 11, 2002

CNN/Money.com
Alexandra Twin, *Strong Brew,* November 8, 2002

Worth Magazine
Caroline Waxler, *Sex Appeal,* November 2002

Business 2.0
Evelyn Nussenbaum, *Skimming from the Wages of Sin,* November 2002

Introduction

The Washington Times
Chris Baker, *Vice Fund Will Not Repent for Investing in "Sin,"* October 29, 2002

Houston Chronicle
Bob Fernandez, *Exploiting the Profits of Vice,* October 14, 2002

Barron's
Jacqueline Doherty, *The Wagers of Sin: Will the Vice Fund Lead Down the Road to Perdition?*, October 7, 2002

ABC News: *Good Morning America*
Dan Harris, *The Bottom Line: Sin Stocks Are Heating Up,* October 2, 2002

Financial Times
Julie Earle and Florian Gimbel, *Vice Funds Play Devil's Advocate by Making Winners Out of "Sinners,"* October 1, 2002

SmartMoney
Eleanor Laise, *Street Smart: Sex Sells, So Why Not Invest in It?*, October 2002

Salt Lake Tribune
Bob Fernandez, *Set Conscience Aside and Rake In Profit with Vice Fund,* September 24, 2002

Time
Bill Barol, *Investing in Bad Habits,* September 23, 2002

Investing in Vice

The Star-Ledger (Newark, N.J.)
Bob Fernandez, *The Vice Section: This Is Not a Fund for Peaceniks, Teetotalers, or Granolas,* September 22, 2002

The Miami Herald
Bob Fernandez, *Vice Fund: "Call Me Irresponsible,"* September 17, 2002

Dow Jones International News
Brian Truscott, *The Skeptic: Global Tensions Make Vice Look Nice, Right?,* September 17, 2002

CNNfn
Bruce Francis and Kathleen Hays, *Money and Markets, Building Your Portfolio,* September 16, 2002

Fortune
Andy Serwer, *Vice Is Nice: For Marketing,* September 16, 2002

Dallas Observer
Patrick Williams, *Buzz: Growth Industries,* September 12, 2002

Hartford Courant
Brendan Sullivan, *Fund Offers Chance to Invest on the Wild Side,* September 10, 2002

Denver Post
Daily Record (Morris County, N.J.) *Vice Is Nice for Dallas-Based Mutual Fund,* September 9, 2002

The New York Times
Jeff Sommer, *Against the Grain at the Vice Fund,* September 8, 2002

Introduction

Financial Times
Julie Earle, *Global Investing: Sugar, Spice, and Most Things Nice Take a Tumble,* September 6, 2002

American Banker
Thomson Financial, *In Brief: New Fund Firm's Portfolio of Vice,* September 5, 2002

St. Louis Post-Dispatch
From Wire Reports, *New Fund Would Make Virtue of Vice,* September 4, 2002

Los Angeles Times
Kathy O'Donnell, *Vice Fund Hopes Cigarettes, Booze Pay Off,* September 3, 2002

The Boston Globe
Alex Beam, *Call for Philip Morris,* September 3, 2002

The Rush Limbaugh Show
Rush Limbaugh, *Vice Fund Launches,* September 3, 2002

Philadelphia Inquirer
Bob Fernandez, *Socially Irresponsible Fund to Go on Sale to Public,* September 3, 2002

Investment News
Frank Kelly, David Hoffman and Bruce Kelly, *Short Interests: Candy Is Dandy, but Liquor's Upticker,* September 2, 2002

Daily Record (Morris County, N.J.)
Warren Boroson, *Others Buy Nice; This Fund Buys Vice,* September 1, 2002

Investing in Vice

South Florida Sun-Sentinel
Kathy O'Donnell, *Vice Fund's Contrarian Appeal: It Flouts Political Correctness,* September 1, 2002

The Press-Enterprise (Riverside, Calif.)
Jonathan Shikes, *Vice Is Nice for Fund Firm,* August 31, 2002

The Independent (London)
Hilary Morison, *Personal Finance: Just How Green Do You Want to Make Your Ethical Investments?,* August 31, 2002

Standard & Poor's Advisor Insight
Palash R. Ghosh, *Fund in Focus: Vice Fund,* August 30, 2002

Financial Times
Julie Earle, *FT Fund Management: Fund Finds Virtue in Vice,* August 29, 2002

Wall Street Journal Online
Erin Schulte, *New Specialty Fund Is Betting on Smoking, Drinking, and Gambling "Sin Stocks,"* August 27, 2002

The Daily Telegraph (London)
Simon English, *The Vice Fund Aims for Rewards in This Life,* August 27, 2002

CNN/Money.com
Paul R. La Monica, *Beer? Yes. Sex? No. The Vice Fund Is Targeting Sinful Stocks,* August 27, 2002

Dallas Business Journal
William Hoffman, *New Fund: Vice Is Nice,* August 26, 2002

Introduction

Mutual Fund Market News
Tony Lystra, *New Vice Fund Invests in "All Things Bad,"* August 26, 2002

TheStreet.com
Beverly Goodman, *A Weakness for "Sin" Stocks,* August 24, 2002

National Business Review
Michael Coote, *On the Money: The Virtues of Vice, a Socially Irresponsible Fund for Investors,* August 23, 2002

Investor's Business Daily
Ken Hoover, *New Fund Seeks Gains in "Sin" Sectors,* August 23, 2002

CBS MarketWatch
Craig Tolliver, *Vice Fund Politically Incorrect/Socially Irresponsible,* August 22, 2002

Forbes.com
James Paton, *"Socially Irresponsible" Fund Pitches to Investors,* August 15, 2002

Wall Street Journal
Theo Francis and Tom Lauricella, *Wages of Sin,* June 5, 2002

Investing in Vice will introduce readers to the concept of investing in so-called sin stocks, all the companies that judgmental moralists would say we should avoid. I contend that the personal freedoms of drinking, smoking, and gambling are woven into the very fabric of American society. Many of our country's founding fathers were drinkers and tobacco farmers. Patriotism and support for our military (and the entire aerospace and defense industry) are near all-time highs.

Investing in Vice will examine each of the primary areas that socially responsible investors avoid: alcohol, gambling, tobacco, adult entertainment, and defense, listing publicly traded stocks and giving descriptions of the most dominant corporations, as well as providing a few "top picks" either of stocks we already own that have performed well or stocks that I believe will perform well in the future.

1

Invest in What You Know

It has been my experience that folks who have no vices have very few virtues.

—Abraham Lincoln

Every enterprise has its superstars and icons, those people to whom everyone else in the business looks up to. In basketball, it might be Michael Jordan. In baseball, Barry Bonds. In golf, Tiger Woods. In art, Rembrandt and Picasso. In literature, Shakespeare and Fitzgerald. In the corporate world, it's men like Lee Iacocca and Jack Welch. And in investing, it's Warren Buffett and Peter Lynch.

The general public might not know too much about Buffett and Lynch, but if you're interested in how to best invest your money, you should learn something about these enormously successful men and how they approach their business.

Investing in Vice

Warren Buffett: Financial Prodigy

Warren Edward Buffett displayed an aptitude for business by the time he was six. A prodigy of sorts, he had already developed the ability to calculate columns of numbers off the top of his head. He also displayed his entrepreneurial resourcefulness early when, as legend has it, he purchased six-packs of Coca-Cola from his grandfather's grocery store for twenty-five cents and then resold the individual bottles for a nickel a piece, thereby earning himself a neat 20 percent profit. Five years later, at the ripe old age of eleven, he purchased three shares of Cities Service Preferred stock at $38 a share. The stock dropped to $27, but then rebounded to $40, at which time the young Buffett sold his stake, pocketing a nifty profit. Unfortunately for Buffett, the stock then shot up to $200. But what he lost in profit he gained in a valuable investing lesson, which was the virtue of patience.

By the mid-1950s, Buffett, along with seven limited partners, including his sister and an aunt, created Buffett Associates. By the end of that first year, while working out of his own bedroom, he was managing close to $300,000 in capital. Within the next five years, Buffett's company showed an eye-popping 251 percent profit, and by 1962, the partnership had capital in excess of $7.2 million. By the mid-1960s, the Buffett partnership's assets were up more than 1,156 percent, as compared to the Dow Jones Industrial Average gain of about 123 percent for the same period.

It wasn't long before Wall Street noted Buffett's amazing successes, and as a result it wasn't unusual for a stock price to shoot up ten points simply based on a rumor that Buffett was going to buy the stock. By the early 1980s, his company, now called Berkshire Hathaway, was trading at close to $300 a share and his personal wealth was in the neighborhood of $140 million. By the 1990s, the stock sold for as high as $80,000 a share.

When the late 1990s rolled around, Buffett, unlike many of

his colleagues, did not get caught up in the dot-com frenzy. This caused some on Wall Street to question his ability to stay in touch with contemporary economics. But Buffett, confident that the technology bubble would burst, continued to invest in great businesses that were selling below their intrinsic value. And once the demise of the dot-coms came, and the market began to freefall, Warren Buffett was once again hailed as an investment wizard.

Buffett's "secret" to investing was actually quite simple. He was most interested in how a company worked and why it was better than any other company in its field. He refused to invest in companies he didn't understand. He had to know what they did and how they did it and how successful they were at doing it before he was willing to invest his money. And his strategy paid off.

Peter Lynch: Corporate Earnings Drive Prices

Peter Lynch, now vice chairman of Fidelity Management and Research Company, is in much the same mold as Warren Buffett. He first rose to prominence as a result of his success as manager of the Fidelity Magellan Fund (FMAGX), the mutual fund he ran from 1977 to 1990. When Lynch first took over the helm, the fund had $20 million in assets. By 1983, the fund's assets were more than $1 billion. In his book *One Up on Wall Street,* Lynch makes his stock-picking strategy very clear: Invest in what you know. He made no attempt to figure out how a complicated industry worked, simply because it was anointed by the media as being "hot." Instead, he invested in industries he already understood and he held fast to the notion that corporate earnings drive stock prices.

For instance, in the early 1980s, Chrysler was near bankruptcy. Most investors and their advisers were avoiding the company like the plague. But Lynch did his homework and was impressed with the prototypes of a new automobile called a mini-van. As a result, he made Chrysler one of Magellan's top holdings and, while his fund owned Chrysler, the stock more than tripled in price.

Lynch's formula is simple yet devastatingly effective. He looks for three qualities in a good company: profitability, price, and a good business model. For instance, in the late 1980s a new fast food company, Au Bon Pain (a division of Panera Bread Company), opened its doors and Lynch pounced on it as an investment because it was offering "quality" fast food rather than "mediocre" fast food.

Lynch's modus operandi is best illustrated by a story he tells in his book. After his wife pointed out that Hanes had begun selling their L'eggs pantyhose in grocery stores, Lynch realized that the company had a clever marketing plan and he purchased the stock for his fund. His prescience was rewarded when Hanes's stock rose six-fold during the time that Magellan held it.

When Lynch retired from Magellan in 1990, the fund had an average total return of 25 percent a year. And remember, this was well before the dot-com boom of the late 1990s.

The Rules of Investment

From both these investment masters, we can learn at least two rules about how to invest successfully: buy what you understand and corporate profits drive stock prices. If you can't understand how a business runs, how it makes its money, or why a company's business model is sound—as many people couldn't during the Internet boom—then it's probably not a good idea to invest in that company.

While in the midst of a recession, it's still the job of money managers to search for good investments for our clients. We're constantly studying different sectors, industries, and investment types, while trying to keep our eyes on the long-term investment horizon. Without suddenly and foolishly putting a client's money into bonds or money markets, my firm began to look for some investments that were, in a manner of speaking, recession proof. What could those be and how could we find them?

Well, as with a lot of things, they were right under our noses. Certain habits, even during bad economic times, don't change. No matter what the stock market is doing, people still indulge in what are known as vices: smoking, drinking, and gambling. So, I wondered, why not look into these so-called vice industries as possible investments?

Of course, this is nothing new. Brokers have often joked about comparing these kinds of investments to the socially responsible investment funds that have sprouted up in the past decade or so. In early 2002, our casual, throwaway jokes suddenly turned into "what ifs," and then, as "what ifs" often do, into some serious research of the fund concept. I conducted a close examination of all the socially responsible funds and all the areas they screen out. I looked at the long-term histories and stock performance of the alcohol, tobacco, and gaming industries. I studied individual companies that were industry leaders such as Anheuser-Busch, Altria, and Harrah's Entertainment. I looked at mutual funds that had large alcohol, gaming, and tobacco holdings and found some very good ones, but I could not find a single mutual fund that was investing solely in these "sin stock" areas.

As I moved forward many people debated the notion of setting up such an investment, discussing many of the pros and cons. Besides all the details of holdings, registrations, expenses, regulatory filings, research data, and distribution, we talked a lot about potential performance and possible public reaction. As for performance, I felt that as a group, these vice industries could always show solid, fairly consistent returns. The bad periods wouldn't be "technology bad." All investment categories under-perform at one time or another. It's inevitable. But I felt that the lows in these industries wouldn't be as bad as the lows the over-all market experiences, and that most years would provide good, positive returns.

Today, I believe that many investors, with the tech boom and bust still fresh in their memory, are a little wiser, their expecta-tions a little more reasonable. Instead of a series of "killings" in the market, they are simply searching for positive but not neces-sarily spectacular returns.

Back to the Future

Today's investors understand that they ought to be looking for slow, steady, "boring" returns again. The go-go days of Wall Street should be behind us. Alcohol, tobacco, gaming, and defense, like household products made by companies like Proc-tor and Gamble and Colgate-Palmolive, are all old-line, old-economy types of stocks that I believe will do well through thick and thin.

The bottom line is, invest in what you know. People have inti-mate knowledge of their so-called bad habits. This is something that every investor can understand. And these "bad" habits are not about to suddenly disappear. People are always going to drink alcohol. People are always going to smoke. People are always going to gamble. This country is always going to be con-cerned about our national security. No matter what happens to the economy I believe that "sin" stocks will thrive. When I came up with the idea of a "vice portfolio," I felt that the public's reaction would be positive because it was something, as Warren Buffett and Peter Lynch might say, they could understand.

Invest in What You Know

The Sin Stocks

The definition of *sin stock* is somewhat open to conjecture. In some cases, it's simply those stocks that are "screened" by the socially responsible funds, which often include alcohol, tobacco, gaming, defense, and weapons as well as those industries that are involved in animal testing, don't meet the rules of being environmentally friendly, have a real or perceived problem with human rights, labor relations, employment equality, and community investment—all of which require some kind of moral judgment.

Obviously, this is a very broad spectrum of industries, and many of them won't be dealt with here.

But before I do introduce the sin stocks that I'm interested in as investments, we ought to discuss the difference between publicly traded and privately traded companies.

After I came up with the idea of investing in vice stocks, I found myself constantly asked questions like, "Do you invest in prostitution in Nevada?" Or, "Do you invest in pornography?" The answer is no, because these are very rarely publicly traded companies—most are either private companies or partnerships. Generally speaking, the majority of what most of us would consider pornography is not available as a publicly traded stock. (Playboy Enterprises, for instance, is a publicly traded stock, but today the general public does not consider that magazine hardcore pornography.)

- Alcohol—Examples of alcohol stocks are Anheuser-Busch (BUD) and Diageo (DEO). Many people aren't familiar with the Diageo name, but it owns famous brands such as Guinness, Seagram's, Smirnoff, and Johnnie Walker.

- Gaming—These stocks include the large casinos like Harrah's Entertainment (HET) and MGM Mirage (MGG), as well as lottery industry stocks like GTECH (GTK), which runs many of the state lotteries, and gaming technology stocks, such as Shuffle Master (SHFL) or International Game Technology (IGT). Gaming is expanding rapidly, state by state.

- Tobacco—These stocks are dominated by some very large players, including Philip-Morris (MO), now called Altria Group, and smokeless tobacco company UST, Inc. (UST). International tobacco companies are also very important and include British American Tobacco, available in the United States as an American Depository Receipt, or ADR (BTI), and Imperial Tobacco, another ADR (ITY).

- Defense—Although defense stocks are not really considered vice or sin stocks, many socially responsible funds screen out all defense and weapons makers. Unfortunately for investors, this also means eliminating all of the aerospace industry, including companies like Lockheed Martin (LMT), L-3 Communications (LLL), United Technologies (UTX), which also makes Otis elevators and Carrier air conditioners, and Northrop Grumman (NOC), which is the Forbes 2003 Company of the Year.

- Adult entertainment—many socially responsible funds attempt to screen out anything having to do with adult entertainment or pornography. The problem with this is that it's difficult to know who is actually making the money or who actually owns the company behind the pornography. And, as I pointed out before, Playboy may or may not be considered pornography. In addition, I've found numerous publicly traded stocks that don't appear to have anything to do with adult entertainment but derive great revenues through cable television or hotel pay-per-view entertainment.

2

Socially Irresponsible Investing

You can't handle the truth!

—Colonel Nathan Jessup, *A Few Good Men*

Socially responsible investing is a hoax. In theory, it's a wonderful, even laudable concept—who wouldn't want to be socially responsible? But in practice it's a mess and is in my opinion an almost useless concept that is misleading millions of investors worldwide.

The notion of socially responsible investing, which means taking your personal beliefs and values and applying them to the way you invest your money, is nothing new. Over a century and a half ago the Quakers, for instance, stood the high moral ground and refused to invest in slavery. During the Vietnam War, protesters raged against companies like Dow Chemical as well as some of the weapons makers, urging investors not to put their money in these giant corporations. And in the late 1970s, during the height of the anti-Apartheid movement in South

Africa and around the world, investors were urged to divest their holdings in multinational corporations that did business in that country.

In the past two decades or so, however, the idea of investing money only in companies that are screened to meet what's called a "double bottom line," that is, being profitable but also adhering to certain moral criteria, has grown enormously in popularity.

The proof is in the numbers. In 1984, $40 billion was invested in socially responsible companies, and by 1999, this figure had risen to a whopping $2.16 trillion of the $16.3 trillion in professionally managed funds in the United States. Another calculation from the Social Investment Forum, an industry trade association, says that in 1997 about $1.2 trillion (or about one-tenth of all institutional investment dollars in the United States at the time) were subject to some kind of screening process.

What this means is that socially responsible investors, either acting on their own or through socially responsible mutual funds, actively screen companies for those holdings that conflict with their beliefs. Some investors refuse to put their money into companies that pollute the environment, use animals for research purposes, or tap into people's vices, such as drinking, smoking, and gaming.

Some investors even go even a little further and screen their investments according to their personal causes. Several years ago, when Ellen DeGeneres had her TV persona declare that she was a lesbian (echoing what DeGeneres had done some time earlier in real life) many conservative and religious groups called for a boycott of what they termed gay-friendly Disney (the parent company that produced the show), which included not only their stock but their theme parks, TV shows, and movies. At the other end of the spectrum, the Meyers Pride Value Fund invested only in companies that offered benefits for gay partners as well as policies that prohibited discrimination against homosexuals.

Socially Irresponsible Investing

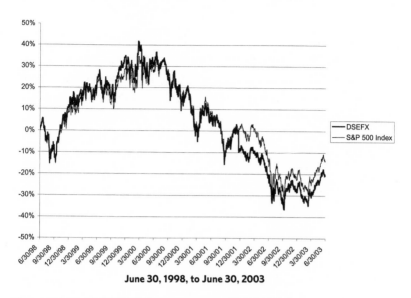

June 30, 1998, to June 30, 2003

Figure 2.1. Domini (DSEFX) returns versus S&P 500 Index.

A large portion of so-called socially responsible investments, or SRI, are in the form of index funds (such as the Domini Social Equity Fund) that screen out tobacco, alcohol, gaming, aerospace, defense, and nuclear power. What's left? All the other publicly traded stocks, but in particular, technology stocks. If a regular index fund owns all stocks within a certain criterion, and an SRI fund owns all those stocks minus the old-line, conservative, dividend-paying tobacco, alcohol, aerospace, and nuclear utility stocks, then the SRI index fund ends up with a larger percentage of its assets in tech stocks. If you want to buy a technology fund, then buy one. But don't be fooled into buying a tech-heavy socially responsible fund for all the wrong reasons.

Over the past five years, Domini's fund, one of the world's largest SRI funds, has practically mirrored the Standard & Poor's 500 Index (see Figure 2.1). Investors certainly aren't gaining any investment return through the fund's screening process. Their weighting toward tech stocks undoubtedly causes the slight five-year underperformance through June 2003.

Generally speaking, funds that consider themselves socially responsible screen from among the following industries:

- tobacco

- gaming

- alcohol

- defense and aerospace

Instead, they may look to invest in companies that have:

- a good environmental record

- supported acceptable human rights practices

- supported labor issues

Or that have taken a stance on:

- abortion or birth control

- animal rights issues

Socially Irresponsible Investing

Today, there are almost two hundred of these socially responsible investment funds. Some of these funds are more strict than others and therein lies one of the problems with this approach to investing. For instance, if a company buys supplies or has other dealings with another company that is on your unacceptable list, should they also be banned as an investment possibility? And what about corporations like McDonald's or Krispy Kreme, whose products may taste good but are not particularly healthful? Which brings up what should be an obvious question in these days of large conglomerates with their hands in numerous businesses: Can any company today be considered 100 percent clean in terms of being socially responsible?

The fact is, there is a good deal of hypocrisy and double talk in the SRI industry, as many funds directly contradict each other as to what "socially responsible" means. Companies that are included in a gay rights SRI mutual fund may also be large holdings in a Catholic values fund. And the ambiguity goes even further. Recently, New York City Mayor Michael Bloomberg extended a smoking ban to all restaurants and bars. And yet it's estimated that the city will make nearly $20 million a year from tobacco investments since the city owns nearly 7.5 million shares of Altria, the company that controls tobacco giant Philip Morris. This despite the fact that a representative for the city comptroller said that since 1998, the New York City pension system has restricted purchasing additional tobacco stocks.

Some funds hold themselves under the SRI umbrella, but seem to have no consistency in their investment philosophy, actually holding stocks such as Altria, Lockheed Martin, and Anheuser-Busch. They claim to be only "influencing" these companies.

Many investors brought in under the socially responsible ideal would be disappointed if they truly understood how their money was managed. While individual investors are simply trying to do the right thing, socially responsible money managers are taking in investor dollars and making money for themselves (as any manager does) while preaching that they are somehow "changing the world."

In addition, some investors in these funds are excessively expensed in a number of ways. While some SRI funds are no-load, many are loaded with 4 percent or 5 percent sales commissions. Among the worst of the lot, in my opinion, is a judgmental family of funds called The Timothy Plan. Their investing philosophy is somewhere along the lines of "What would St. Timothy do?" They claim that they're against abortion, pornography, antifamily entertainment, unmarried lifestyles, alcohol, tobacco, and gambling. Unless they have some type of direct conduit through God, I don't think they know exactly what St. Timothy would do. One thing that I think St. Timothy would *not do* is charge a fat 5.5 percent commission on the front end of their A-shares. I don't think the biblical Timothy was in the commission business.

The huge Calvert Fund family charges a 4.75 percent front-end sales load on the majority of their funds. Another, called the New Alternatives Fund also charges a large 4.75 percent on the front end. Parnassus Fund, 3.5 percent up front. And many of these funds have very high total expense ratios, cutting into investor returns. The religion-based Noah Fund takes a high 2.2 percent internal expense ratio. Green Century Balanced, an outrageous 2.39 percent. Many other socially responsible funds follow closely behind with above-average expenses. Where's the money going? I don't know. Could it be flowing to many levels of highly compensated boards, advisory panels, or fund managers? One has to wonder.

Socially Irresponsible Investing

Under the Microscope: SRI Funds Unmasked

If you take a little closer look at some of the components of these SRI funds you'll find some interesting anomalies. For example, among the major stocks recently owned in the Domini Social Equity Fund are Atlantic Richfield (Arco), Bell Atlantic, Intel, Mattel, Merck, Microsoft, and Wal-Mart. Arco drills for oil in the Alaskan wilderness; Intel and Microsoft have been assailed as vicious monopolies; Intel has been accused of polluting; Merck is involved in patenting genetic material from the world's rain forests; the superstores of Wal-Mart have been criticized for crushing smaller mom-and-pop store competition, selling guns and Kathie Lee Gifford's clothing line, which was denounced by activists for using child labor in Honduras. And recently, Wal-Mart has been accused of discriminating against women in its employment practices.

The Parnassus Fund has also owned shares in Intel, as well as Toys "R" Us, which the Federal Trade Commission found guilty of price-fixing and forcing toy manufacturers into exclusive sales agreements.

And finally, Citizens Growth Fund owned stock in Saks Fifth Avenue. According to *Free Market* commentator James M. Sheehan, after the fund found that the giant department store chain was using textiles made in Chinese prison camps under the control of the People's Liberation Army, the fund simply asked Saks to sign a list of "anti-sweatshop principles."

Even the legendary consumer advocate Ralph Nader is guilty of some form of hypocrisy. When he was running for president, he revealed that he had over $3 million invested in stocks—a substantial part through Fidelity Magellan—and among his recent holdings were Cisco Systems, Occidental Petroleum, Raytheon (a missile manufacturer), ExxonMobil, BP-Amoco and Bristol-Myers Squibb.

Investing in Vice

99 and 99/100th Percent Pure?

So, exactly how pure are these socially responsible funds?

Not very.

According to Doug Henwood, editor of the *Left Business Observer*, there is no possible way to invest responsibly and still earn a good return on your money. Instead, you must simply bite the bullet and purchase a regular mutual fund while realizing "that what you're doing is unethical." Henwood actually takes a more moderate approach. Instead of "doing well by doing good," he advises, "do well by not doing such pure bad."

But as far as I'm concerned, all this is beside the point. Once again, the purpose of investing is to make money.

I believe that people should donate their time and money to good causes they believe in, but I don't think they should vote with their investments. I think they should invest to make money, not to make a political statement.

Besides, don't we already have laws that protect employment and human rights? Don't we already have laws that protect the environment against pollution and protect against child labor?

Of course we do, and these laws should be vigilantly enforced and even enhanced. But do we really need socially responsible investment managers to protect us from evil in these areas? Is it really part of their job description?

The answer to both questions is a resounding no. It might be different if we were talking about international or emerging markets mutual funds, but the bulk of socially responsible investing is U.S. based and invested in U.S. companies.

Socially responsible investors would say that you shouldn't own stocks that have anything to do with defense or weapons and that means that all of the aerospace and defense industries should be avoided. Maybe in a perfect world these industries wouldn't need to exist, but until that perfect world does exist,

Socially Irresponsible Investing

I'd want to own these stocks and I think you should, too. And besides, who is to say what companies behave ethically and what companies don't? A few years ago, everyone was buying Enron stock. Do you think most people really understood the business Enron was in? WorldCom and HealthSouth are two other great examples of how perceptions can be very misleading, and investors can be led down a confusing path.

The lesson is obvious: Don't be too quick to judge good companies versus bad. For instance, socially responsible investors might well shun buying stock in Anheuser-Busch because it sells alcohol. But Anheuser-Busch isn't evil incarnate. In fact, I believe that the company is a great corporate citizen. To my knowledge, no one is accusing it of "cooking the books." Among other things, the company has been recycling for more than a hundred years. In fact, it recycles more than 97 percent of the waste it generates.

In addition:

- Anheuser-Busch Recycling Corporation (ABRC) is the world's largest recycler of used aluminum beverage containers. In 2002, it recycled 776 million pounds, more than 125 percent of the number of cans its own breweries used to package their product.

- Busch Agriculture Resource operations composted more than 619 million pounds of farm materials in 2002. The company saved more than 1.3 million pounds of aluminum and 10.5 million pounds of paperboard by modifying its packaging.

- Anheuser-Busch's graphics department has implemented the use of recycled paper for company letterhead, business cards, and envelopes. It also uses agriculture-based inks, rather than petroleum-based products.

Investing in Vice

The bottom line is this: There's nothing wrong with social investing if it helps you sleep at night. But I think investing should be done to make money. You can donate your profits if you want. But don't invest to make a political statement. Corporations that are truly doing evil are poor investments on their own merits—I don't seek to invest in them. But again, who's to judge what is truly evil?

3

Alcohol: I'll Drink to That

His biographers declare that in eating and in
drinking as in all things, [George Washington] was
normal; enjoying the juice of the malt all the days of
his life. He drank it around campfires, as well as in
his own home and upon social and state occasions.

—Magazine ad, Anheuser-Busch Archives

If, as an investor, you are to follow the sage advice offered by Peter Lynch and Warren Buffet, you needn't look any further than around the corner, to your favorite neighborhood watering hole. Chances are, that by six o'clock in the evening the bar is three or four deep, filled with folks who just an hour or two earlier were toiling away at their desks, looking forward to happy hour to unwind from an arduous day at work. Or, check out the commercials during any major televised sporting event and you'll find a plethora of ads featuring gorgeous women being impressed by even the geekiest guy who's holding onto a bottle of Bud or Coors or Heineken or Corona.

No matter the state of the economy, whether we're in a recession or a boom, people drink. They don't stop drinking when the Dow Jones drops (in fact, they might even drink a little more), and they don't stop drinking when the Dow Jones goes through the roof (they might drink more to celebrate). And so, why wouldn't an investor want to put money into the alcohol industry?

The State of the Industry

The alcoholic beverage industry in this country is a highly profitable business. Although in recent years the growth of net sales as been relatively slow, at only 2 percent to 4 percent a year, profitability as measured by operating margins is quite high as compared to most other consumer goods. Standard & Poor's estimates that average operating margins for U.S. alcoholic beverage companies are about 20 percent, which is well above the 12 percent to 14 percent that is the typical average operating margin for packaged food companies.

The health of the alcoholic beverage industry (and this is also true of the tobacco industry, discussed in chapter 5) is distinguished by three major characteristics:

1. Degree of concentration

2. High profitability

3. High barriers to entry

Over the years, the alcohol industry has undergone considerable consolidation due, in part, to a trend of declining domestic consumption and a maturing marketplace. The result of this consolidation is that breaking into the domestic market is very difficult, and the stronger companies, like Anheuser-Busch, have abnormally high profit margins, excellent cash flow, and high investment returns.

Although the major companies in the alcoholic beverage industry currently face some resistance to domestic growth, the stronger companies have reorganized their business structures via acquisitions or restructurings, while at the same time they have vigorously pursued the more rapidly growing international markets. As another way of maximizing profits, industry leaders continuously engage in new product development.

Another factor that makes the alcoholic beverage industry an attractive investment is that the number of consumers reaching legal drinking age has been on a steady upswing in recent years. For instance, beginning in 1999, the twenty-one to twenty-four-year-old age group started to grow for the first time since the 1970s. Thanks to this increase in legal age drinkers, the industry expects an additional 1 percent annual gain in beer sales in the years ahead. Beer, after all, has traditionally been the alcoholic beverage of choice for drinkers in their early twenties.

According to the Beer Institute, the trade association that represents the malt beverage industry, Americans drank on average about 21.3 gallons of malt beverages in 2001. And the amount of beer shipped to wholesalers has increased steadily over the past five years, topping out at a little over 200 million 31-gallon barrels in 2001.

While the under twenty-five crowd is multiplying, so are the baby boomers, who now constitute the over-fifty-five age group. This rapidly growing demographic bodes well for increasing the sales of their alcoholic beverages of choice: wines and spirits.

Another sign of the overall health of the industry has to do with the attitude of state governments across the country. In the past, most states and municipalities had strict blue laws, which prohibited the sale of alcohol at particular times and in particular places. But in the last twenty years, these laws have either been modified or cleared from the books. For instance, in spring 2003, Governor Ruth Ann Minner of Delaware signed a law allowing Sunday liquor store sales from noon to 8 P.M. It is estimated that allowing Sunday sale of alcohol will raise the small state's annual alcoholic beverage tax revenues from $960,000 to $1.2 million.

Other states have also jumped on the bandwagon.

- In 2002, Oregon, a state with one of the nation's deepest deficits, passed a law allowing Sunday liquor sales.

- In spring 2003, the New York State Legislature voted to allow Sunday sales, provided the stores closed another, potentially slower, day of the week.

- In early 2003, Pennsylvania began allowing Sunday sales at sixty-one of its six-hundred-plus state-owned stores. There's talk of allowing all the stores to stay open Sundays two years from now.

- The state laws could also be dropped or relaxed soon in Kansas, Rhode Island, and Washington.

- Four of the five most populous states (Texas is the exception) now allow liquor stores to open on Sundays.

Expanding Horizons

Since the population of the United States is growing only at the rate of about 1 percent annually, the domestic market for alco-

Alcohol: I'll Drink to That

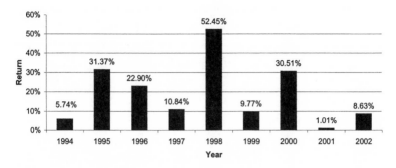

Figure 3.1. BUD yearly stock returns, 1993–2003.

holic beverages is limited. However, this has simply forced the leaders in the industry to look beyond our shores, where the population is rising at a much faster rate. According to projections made by the Department of Commerce, the world's developing countries are expanding at a much faster rate than developed countries. Fifty years ago, about two thirds of the world's population was based in less developed countries. Today, that figure has grown to almost 80 percent, with most of the world's population growth coming from Africa, Asia, and Latin America.

The American alcoholic beverage industry is adapting well to this situation by going after the potential profits to be found in the developing markets of Latin American, Eastern Europe, and Asia. American companies have started exporting their products and have also pursed joint ventures with local brewers and distributors.

Anheuser-Busch, the world's largest beer maker, has been the most aggressive company in developing these emerging markets. In the past ten years, the company has put together deals in Brazil, Japan, India, Italy, France, China, Switzerland, and Spain.

In fact, Anheuser-Busch is a symbol of the overall health of the industry. Every year, since 1993, the company has shown positive stock returns. (See Figure 3.1 on page 35.) The Standard & Poor's 500 Index, by comparison, returned approximately −9.1 percent in 2000, −11.9 percent in 2001, and −22.1 percent in 2002.

A Brief History of Alcohol

Although the production of alcoholic spirits like gin and brandy can only be traced back one thousand or so years, alcohol has been central to social, religious, and personal use all over the world throughout history. In fact, one of the earliest mentions of wine making is from an Egyptian papyrus dated 3500 B.C.

The ancient Egyptians and Chinese brewed beer, as did pre-Columbian civilizations in the Americas who used corn instead of the usual barley. In the Middle Ages, European monks were involved in the making of beer, refining the process and institutionalizing the use of hops as a flavoring and preservative. The arduous process, which included brewers having to depend on wild, airborne yeast for fermentation, took a giant leap forward when Louis Pasteur established that yeast is a living microorganism, thereby giving brewers the power to control the conversion of sugar to alcohol.

Due to the cooler climate, the northern European countries, like Germany and England, became noted for their beer production (barley grows better in cooler climates), while the warmer climate countries, like Italy and Spain, became better known for their wines (grapes grow better in warmer climates).

Over the years, Britain has had its share of alcohol-related problems. Between 1720 and 1750 the so-called gin epidemic was in full swing, when distillers were busy making the strongest and cheapest spirits they could. Because of the great number of deaths related to this "epidemic," Parliament passed an act in 1751 putting a high tax on spirits of particularly high alcohol content.

The industrial revolution caused an upsurge in alcohol use because many people saw it as the ideal way to escape the boredom and pain of their urban working lives.

In America, alcohol quickly became an important part of the fabric of the country, starting with the Pilgrims who carried with them an ample supply of English ale. The first record of the existence of a public brewery in the Massachusetts Bay area dates back to 1638, but prior to this, tavern-keepers brewed small batches of ale themselves. In fact, Americans drank more alcohol per person during the colonial period than any other time in our history.

The brewing of alcoholic beverages was considered important enough that only voters and church members could obtain the right to brew and sell beer. Samuel Adams, one of the revolutionary forefathers, was a brewer himself, as were many prominent revolutionary generals.

The local tavern-keeper was held in very high esteem, as evidenced by the opening paragraph of Alice Morse Earle's chapter called "Tavern in War":

> The tavern has ever played an important part in social, political and military life, has helped to make history. From the earliest days when men gathered to talk over the terrors of Indian warfare; through the renewal of these fears in the French and Indian Wars, before and after the glories of Louisburg and through all the anxious but steadfast years preceding and during the Revolution, these gatherings were held in taverns and ordinaries. What a scene took place in the Brookfield Tavern! The only ordinary, that of Goodman Ayres, was a garrison house as well as a tavern and the sturdy landlord was commander of the train band.

In the late eighteenth century, American farmers who distilled whiskey rebelled against the federal government as a result of the Congress's decision to levy a new tax on spirits. In response to what became known as the Whiskey Rebellion, President George Washington led an army of 13,000 into Pennsylvania to quell the protestors.

Years later, the American attitude toward alcoholic beverages was neatly summed up by the legendary frontiersman Davy Crockett, who was, at the time, a congressman from Kentucky: "As Congress allows lemonade to members and it is charged under the head of stationery, I move that whiskey be allowed under the item of fuel."

The beer and alcoholic spirits industry thrived in this country until 1920, when Prohibition took effect. Many breweries went out of business and gangsters took over the distribution of alcoholic beverages, either making the brew themselves or smuggling it in from other countries.

Prohibition proved to be a grave mistake, and in 1931 Congress passed the twenty-first amendment, which repealed Prohibition and once again, the alcoholic beverage industry began to thrive. During Jimmy Carter's presidency, home brewing was legalized and resulted in an explosion of microbreweries around the country.

Performance

The MUTUALS.com studies all vary somewhat from indexes created by Dow Jones, Standard & Poor's, and others. While those firms provide accurate data, I feel that their indices are not truly representative of the entire alcoholic beverage industry, or other industries that we track. As an example, the Dow Jones Distillers & Brewers Index contains only five companies, while

Alcohol: I'll Drink to That

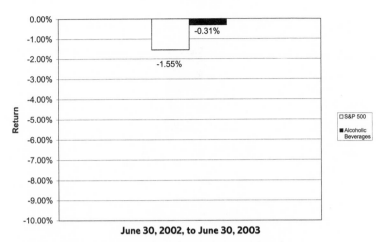

Figure 3.2 One-year return, alcohol versus S&P 500 Index.

we use fifteen. Also, Dow Jones includes U.S.-based companies only, while many top alcohol companies are based overseas. The Dow Jones Tobacco Index contains only three tobacco companies, while we use thirteen.

From June 30, 2002, through June 30, 2003, alcohol was almost flat at −0.31 percent, while the Standard & Poor's 500 returned −1.55 percent. The total three-year return (not annualized) for alcohol was up 32.05 percent, while the S&P 500 lost 33.01 percent total. For five years, alcohol gained a solid 46.02 percent, and the S&P 500 showed a 14.05 percent loss for the full five-year period.

In each of the industry studies conducted by MUTUALS.com, we used the same methodology. We included all of the industry's U.S. publicly traded stocks plus foreign firms traded on the U.S. market. The stocks were market-cap weighted, as are most market indexes such as the Standard & Poor's 500 Index. Market capitalization is simply the market price of the entire company. It's calculated by multiplying the number of shares outstanding by the price

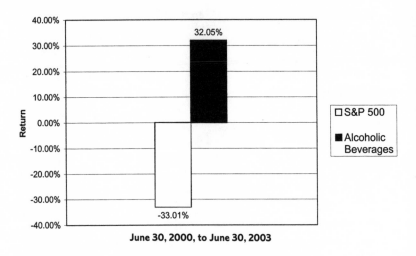

Figure 3.3. Three-year return, alcohol versus S&P 500 Index.

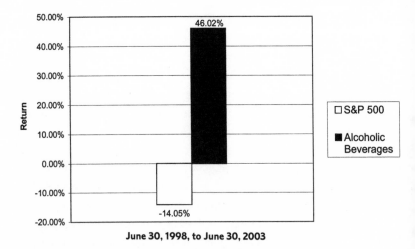

Figure 3.4. Five-year return, alcohol versus S&P 500 Index.

per share. For instance, a company with a $1 billion market capitalization counts ten times as much as a $100 million company. To simplify the analysis, we eliminated all firms with less than $50 million of market cap, because we felt that the very small companies are statistically insignificant. A list of alcohol companies used in the study follows at the end of the chapter in Figure 3.5. In the next section, I'll discuss my favorite stocks in detail.

Top Alcohol Stocks

Generally speaking, I only invest in companies that I expect to hold long term. Short-term price fluctuations are of little concern to me, although a price dip can provide buying opportunities. I am a big believer in the alcohol industry as a whole, and recommend investments in a good, diversified cross section of these stocks, as I have in my portfolio. That said, here are some companies that I particularly like and why.

ANHEUSER-BUSCH (BUD)

Incorporated in 1979, Anheuser-Busch Companies, Inc., is the parent company of Anheuser-Busch, Inc. (ABI), as well as numerous other subsidiaries that conduct a variety of business operations, some—but not all—related to BUD's essential interest: beer.

BUD's operations include the brewing, sales, and marketing of domestic and international beer, beer packaging, family entertainment, and some real estate development. The domestic beer business focuses on manufacturing and wholesale operations, while the company's international segment involves export sales and the production and marketing of beer overseas. BUD's packaging business includes the manufacture of aluminum beverage cans and lids, glass, and crown and closure liner material, as well as aluminum recycling and label printing.

The entertainment segment of the company consists of adventure and theme parks, while other subsidiaries operate a resort and conference center and a transportation service business.

Beer Operations in the United States

BUD's principal product is, of course, beer and malt beverages, sold under a slew of brand names, including: Budweiser, Bud Light, Bud Dry, Bud Ice, Bud Ice Light, Michelob, Michelob Light, Michelob Golden Draft, Michelob Black & Tan Lager, Michelob Hefe-Weizen, Michelob Marzen, Busch, Busch Light, Busch Ice, Natural Light, Natural Ice, King Cobra, Pacific Ridge Ale, Hurricane Malt Liquor, Hurricane Ice, Ziegenbock Amber, Doc's Hard Lemon, and Tequiza. They also offer a few nonalcoholic malt beverages—O'Doul's, O'Doul's Amber, and Busch NA. ABI's newest products include Michelob ULTRA, Bacardi Silver, and American Red, all introduced in 2002. A handful of products—Red Wolf Lager, Red Label, Killarney's, and Doc's Hard Apple—were discontinued by the company at about the same time.

Through an agreement with Japan's Kirin Brewing Company, Ltd., Anheuser-Busch brews and sells Kirin Light, Kirin Lager, and Kirin-Ichiban in the United States. Also, ABI owns a 29.5 percent equity interest in Redhook Ale Brewery, Inc., based in Seattle.

Beer Operations Overseas

Anheuser-Busch International, Inc., one of BUD's wholly owned subsidiaries, oversees the marketing and sale of Budweiser and the company's other brands overseas. The international subsidiary also operates breweries in the United Kingdom and China. International beer volume climbed to almost 8 million barrels in 2002, up from 7.5 million in 2001. Anheuser-Busch beer products are marketed in over 80 countries and U.S. territories.

In several countries, BUD's products are manufactured and sold through license agreements with leading local brewers. Budweiser is brewed and sold under license by Kirin Brewing Company, Limited, in Japan, Oriental Brewery Company in Korea, and Guinness Ireland Ltd., in Ireland and Northern Ireland, as well as by brewers in Italy and Spain. Four BUD offerings—Budweiser, Bud Light, Busch, and Busch Light—are brewed and marketed in Canada by Labatt Brewing Company. In France Budweiser is sold and distributed by a local brewer, Brasseries Kronenbourg.

Packaging Operations

BUD has several subsidiaries that manage the different aspects of the company's packaging operations. Beverage cans and lids are manufactured by Metal Container Corporation, while Anheuser-Busch Recycling Corporation handles the purchase and sale of used beverage containers and is responsible for recycling aluminum cans. Glass bottles for the company's brewery in Houston are made at a glass manufacturing plant in nearby Jacinto City, operated by Longhorn Glass Manufacturing, L.P., a limited partnership owned by BUD. Precision Printing and Packaging, Inc., produces the paper and metalized labels that go on the bottles, and Eagle Packaging, Inc., manufactures crown and closure liner materials.

Investing in Vice

Family Entertainment

Through yet another wholly owned subsidiary, Busch Entertainment Corporation (BEC), Anheuser-Busch is also very active in the area of family entertainment—also known as theme parks. BEC owns and operates Busch Gardens theme parks in Tampa, Florida, and Williamsburg, Virginia. In those same two cities BEC also operates two of its water park attractions—Adventure Island in Tampa and Water Country, United States in Williamsburg. Other BEC water parks include Sesame Place in Langhorne, Pennsylvania, and Discovery Cove in Orlando, Florida—which allows guests to interact with marine animals and operates on a reservations-only system. In addition, BEC is the owner/operator of the three SeaWorld theme parks in Orlando, San Diego, California, and San Antonio, Texas. Finally, BUD also has a hand in family entertainment overseas, indirectly owning a 16.1 percent equity interest in a theme park near Barcelona—Port Aventura, S.A.

Thoughts

BUD is the thousand-pound gorilla of the alcohol industry. It dominates and is likely to continue to dominate the industry. The economies of scale in the alcohol industry make them virtually impossible to beat, leading to increasing domestic market share and great international growth. Their uncanny growth through good times and bad times leads to rising stock prices through thick and thin. I think BUD is also an extremely socially responsible company, recycling more aluminum each year than they use. And they use a lot of aluminum cans.

Alcohol: I'll Drink to That

CONSTELLATION BRANDS (STZ)

Incorporated in 1972, Constellation Brands, Inc., produces and markets a number of alcohol beverage brands in North America and the United Kingdom. In the United States, the company supplies wine, beer, and distilled spirits. In the United Kingdom, the company is a primary marketer of wine and cider. Constellation has four alcohol segments:

1. Imported Beer and Spirits—Constellation imports and markets several varieties of beer; it also produces, bottles, imports, and distributes a number of famous distilled spirits brands. In the United States, the company markets six of the top twenty-five imported beer brands, including Corona Extra, Modelo Especial, Corona Light, Pacifico, St. Pauli Girl, and Negra Modelo. It also imports Tsingtao from China, Peroni from Italy, and Double Diamond and Tetley's English Ale from the United Kingdom. In addition to supplying distilled spirits in the United States, Constellation exports to approximately twenty-five countries around the world. Among the most popular brands of distilled spirits handled by Constellation are Black Velvet, Fleischmann's, Mr. Boston, Canadian LTD, Chi-Chi's prepared cocktails, Montezuma, Barton, Monte Alban, Ten High, and Inver House.

2. Popular and Premium Wines—For both the domestic and export markets, Constellation produces, bottles, imports, and markets table wine, dessert wine, sparkling wine, and brandy. Its brands include Alice White, Almaden, Arbor Mist, Dunnewood, Inglenook, Manischewitz, Marcus James, Paul Masson, Talus, Taylor, Vendange, Vina Santa Carolina, Cook's, J. Roget, Wild Irish Rose, Estate Cellars, and Covey Run.

3. UK Brands and Wholesale—Constellation Brands controls a sizable share of the British fortified wine market through its QC and Stone's brand names. It also has a significant market position in the regular wine category through Babycham, Arbor Mist, and Country Manor. This segment also produces cider brands in the United Kingdom that include Gaymer's Olde English, Blackthorn, Diamond White and K. It's also involved in the bottled water business with the brand Strathmore. The UK Brands and Wholesale segment of Constellation acts as an independent beverage wholesaler throughout the British Isles in the distribution of wine, distilled spirits, cider, beer, and soft drinks.

4. Fine Wine—Constellation's brands include Estancia, Ravenswood, Franciscan Oakville Estate, Simi, Veramonte, Mt. Veeder and Quintessa wines. It exports to approximately twenty-five countries. The company also has its own winery and numerous vineyard holdings in California and Chile.

Thoughts

Constellation Brands is diversified. Premium wine alone is a tough business. Volume is needed for profit margin. Distilled spirits see highs and lows in public demand. To make the most money in beer, you need to compete with BUD and handle everything from ingredients to production, packing, and distribution. Constellation does lots of things well. It won't attempt to compete with BUD in beer production, so it imports some of the top foreign beer brands into the United States. It sells top-label premium wines, but also the cheaper, high-volume stuff. It owns top brands in whiskey, rum, vodka, gin, and tequila. As various alcohol segments go through phases of popularity, Constellation is there to profit.

COMPANHIA DE BEBIDAS AMERICA—AMBEV (ABV)

AmBev is a Latin American brewery with worldwide distribution. It produces, distributes, and sells beer and other beverage products such as soft drinks, iced tea and water, primarily in Brazil. It also controls sizable market share in Argentina, Chile, Uruguay, Venezuela, and Paraguay. In addition, AmBev is the exclusive distributor of Pepsi beverage products in Brazil.

Beer is the company's core business, and AmBev operates eleven beer and fourteen mixed beer/soft drink plants in Brazil. The Company sold its operations in Argentina, Bolivia, Paraguay and Uruguay to Quinsa S.A., another large brewer already doing business in those four countries. As a result of the transaction, AmBev will maintain more than 35 percent voting rights and economic interest in Quinsa.

AmBev's beers are divided into three main beer brands and represent their core products: Skol, Brahma and Antarctica. As is often the case with U.S. brands, each of these brands offers a variety of beers, including pilsner, lager, dark and nonalcoholic beers.

AmBev's soft drink offerings are also a significant source of revenue with such brands as Guarana Antarctica, Pepsi, and Sukita orange soda. AmBev also sells a number of other nonalcoholic beverages such as mineral water, sport drinks, and iced tea.

Thoughts

While few people in the United States are familiar with AmBev, it is practically the BUD of South America. The company dominates the market and, as pointed out earlier in this chapter, that position is more important in alcohol than in almost any other industry. Through its huge South American market share, AmBev is actually the sixth largest beverage company in the world, and Skol is one of the world's top-selling beer brands. While U.S. companies are competing for participation in the fast-growing international markets, AmBev is already a dominant player, right in the middle of the South American population explosion.

FOMENTO ECONOMICO MEXICANO, S.A. DE C.V., ADR (FMX)

Incorporated in 1936, FEMSA is headquartered in Monterrey, Nuevo Leon. It's Mexico's largest producer of beer (accounting for approximately 45 percent of the country's beer market) and soft drinks, and its products are distributed in approximately 270,000 retail stores throughout Mexico.

FEMSA Cerveza, S.A. de C.V., which was originally founded in 1890, produces, distributes, and markets beer. The company's brands include Tecate, Tecate Light, Sol, Dos Equis Lager, Dos Equis Amber, Carta Blanca, Superior, Indio, Bohemia, and Noche Buena, among others. FEMSA's beer brands are exported primarily to the United States, but also to over sixty-five select countries in Latin America, Europe, and Asia.

The company is also a major producer of soft drinks in Mexico and Argentina, maintaining eight bottling plants in Mexico and one in Buenos Aires. One of the company's subsidiaries, Coca-Cola FEMSA, is the bottler for Coca-Cola in Latin America and accounts for approximately 24 percent of all cola sales in Mexico and approximately 24 percent of all cola sales in Argentina. Soft drinks include: Coca-Cola, Coca-Cola Light,

Sprite, Diet Sprite, Fanta, Fresca, Delaware Punch, Schweppes, PowerADE, Ciel, Ciel Mineralizada, Senzao, Tai, Quatro, and Kin.

Through a subsidiary, FEMSA also operates Oxxo, Mexico's largest chain of convenience stores. By the beginning of 2002, Oxxo had nearly two thousand stores strategically located throughout Mexico's most important metropolitan areas. The company hopes to add approximately three hundred new stores in each of the next few years.

Thoughts

I'm a little reluctant to offer almost the same comments for FEMSA as I expressed for BUD and AmBev, lest it seem as if I'm repeating myself, but control of the market, or dominance, is more important in the alcohol business than almost any other. FEMSA is the largest beer producer and distributor in the growing Mexican market. The company also exports a great deal of beer to the United States and Canada. Although there is slow growth in overall U.S. beer consumption, Americans have an increasing appetite for niche beers and imports. Mexicans are amazed that the cheap beer Tecate is viewed as a high-end import in the United States.

FEMSA also has a nice income stream that comes from controlling the distribution of Coca-Cola—the world's most recognized brand name—through a large part of Mexico and Argentina. Like Anheuser-Busch in the United States, FEMSA benefits from controlling much of their market end to end, producing its own cans, bottles, caps, and labels.

Investing in Vice

DIAGEO PLC, ADR (DEO)

Diageo PLC was incorporated in 1997 as a result of a huge merger between GrandMet PLC and Guinness PLC. It's now one of the world's largest alcohol corporations and offers a wide variety of famous international brands. Its primary business is producing and marketing branded premium spirits in approximately two hundred countries, although it has been involved with numerous nonalcohol consumer goods and services. Alcohol brands include Smirnoff vodka, Johnnie Walker Scotch whiskies, Guinness stout, Baileys Original Irish Cream liqueur, J&B Scotch whisky, Captain Morgan rum, and Tanqueray gin. Diageo also brews and sells other companies' beer brands, such as Budweiser and Carlsberg lagers in Ireland, Heineken lager in Jamaica, and Tiger beer in Malaysia.

In the last few years, the company has taken a number of steps to concentrate on the alcohol business. For instance, in late 2001, Diageo sold its packaged food businesses, which produced and distributed food brands such as Old El Paso Mexican foods, Progresso soups, Green Giant vegetables, Pillsbury refrigerated dough, and Haagen-Dazs ice cream, to General Mills, Inc.

At the end of 2001, Diageo, along with Pernod Ricard S.A., acquired the spirits and wine businesses of The Seagram Company Ltd., which included the brands of Captain Morgan rum, Crown Royal Canadian whiskey, Seagram's 7 American whiskey, Seagram's VO Canadian whiskey, Cacique rum, Windsor Premier whisky, Myers's rum, and Sterling Vineyards wine.

Diageo's most recent move to spin off nonalcohol divisions was to sell Burger King to a group comprised of Texas Pacific Group, Bain Capital Partners, and Goldman Sachs in December 2002.

Alcohol: I'll Drink to That

Company (Ticker)	Market Capitalization
Anheuser-Busch Companies (BUD)	$42.9 billion
Diageo PLC (ADR) (DEO)	$35.0 billion
Kirin Brewery Company, Ltd. (KNBWY)	$6.9 billion
Allied Domecq PLC (ADR) (AED)	$6.4 billion
Brown-Forman Corp. (BFB)	$5.6 billion
Quilmes Industrial, S.A. (LQU)	$4.7 billion
Constellation Brands, Inc. (STZ)	$2.8 billion
Adolph Coors Company (RKY)	$1.8 billion
Compania Cervecerias Unid (CU)	$1.1 billion
Companhia de Bebidas Amer (ABV)	$790.8 million
Robert Mondavi Corp. (MOND)	$399.7 million
Boston Beer Company (SAM)	$221.9 million
Central European Distibution (CEDC)	$199.4 million
Chalone Wine Group, Ltd. (CHLN)	$95.4 million
Todhunter International (THT)	$55.8 million

Figure 3.5. List of all alcohol companies with market cap.

Thoughts

If you're committed to the alcohol industry, you almost have to own Diageo. If Anheuser-Busch is representative of the beer side of the business, Diageo represents distilled spirits. It's a solid company that's done a great job of focusing on its core business through a series of acquisitions and divestitures. The company thrives by owning some of the top alcohol brand names, and by consistently marketing them worldwide. It has great economies of scale with truly global marketing campaigns.

Investing in Vice

On an interesting note, Guinness, and its famous worldwide brand name, was a favorite stock of Warren Buffett's Berkshire Hathaway in the 1990s before it was merged into what is now Diageo.

4

Gaming: Place Your Bets

Gambling is inevitable. No matter what is said or done by advocates or opponents in all its various forms, it is an activity that is practiced, or tacitly endorsed, by a substantial majority of Americans.

—Final Report, Commission on the Review of the National Policy Toward Gambling, 1976

It's been more than twenty-five years since the Commission on the Review of the National Policy Toward Gambling issued its findings, which essentially stated the obvious: gambling in America is here to stay.

Over the last three decades, the gaming industry in this country has undergone a tremendous period of growth. Today, the United States has been transformed from a nation where legalized gambling was a limited and relatively rare phenomenon into one in which such activity is commonplace. Las Vegas is one of the world's top family destinations with new multimillion-dollar themed casinos built every year. And virtually everyone in the United States now has access to some form of legalized gambling in their own region of the country.

In the past, gamblers were forced to travel to Nevada or

Atlantic City in New Jersey to place their legal bets. Now, wagers are placed in nearly every state: on riverboats in the Midwest, at Mississippi gulf coast casinos, at dog and horse pari-mutuel tracks across the country, in off-track betting parlors, and in Indian reservation casinos from coast to coast. In addition, although not legal in the United States, Internet gambling is growing rapidly worldwide. And, in an effort not to be left out of the immense possibilities of gaming revenue, state governments have become one of gambling's biggest proponents in the form of various kinds of state lotteries.

In 1976, Americans legally bet $17.3 billion. In 1996, that figure ballooned to an eye-opening $586.5 billion. And, as Timothy L. O'Brien pointed out in his book *Bad Debt,* as a nation, "we lost $47.6 billion gambling legally in 1996, about $14 billion more than New York City's public budget and more than twice as much as the Coca-Cola Company's sales in the same year."

As of today, at least seventeen states allow either full-scale gambling or what are called "racinos," tracks with slot machine parlors attached, and the gross gaming revenues in those states amounted to nearly $28 billion in 2001, which generated tax revenues of about $4 billion. This tax revenue has caused neighboring states to compete with each other for gaming revenue. Maryland has a plan to bring in 10,000 slot machines in an effort to keep its citizens from visiting nearby Delaware and West Virginia for their gaming. In West Virginia, video terminals account for 12 percent of the state government's revenue.

As a result of this potential tax bonanza, other states are considering turning to gaming to solve their budget crises. In New York, for instance, Governor George Pataki recently unveiled a new plan that avoided raising taxes but relied in part on increased gambling revenue by adding as many as forty-five hundred video lottery terminals to three large Off-Track Betting outlets.

Internet gambling is also growing at an incredible pace. In the spring of 2003, Chris Moneymaker, an accountant from the suburbs of Nashville, actually turned a $40 entry fee in an Internet poker tournament into $2.5 million when he won the World Series of Poker's No Limit Texas Hold'em event in Las Vegas. Many people attributed the record field of 839 players, up a third from 2002's event, in large part to the increase in popularity of online poker.

There's no doubt about it, gambling is very big business in America and this was a point brought home to me when, in May 2003, I attended the annual Southern Gaming Expo in Biloxi, Mississippi, where I saw the results of regional gaming expansion firsthand.

Mississippi is a great example of how gaming is catching on in so many states across the country. Again, it's not simply about Vegas and Atlantic City anymore. Now, other states and municipalities are realizing the powerful two-fold impact of gaming: direct tax revenue and the indirect tourism revenue.

Casino gambling was only introduced into Mississippi in 1992 and yet, according to the Mississippi Gaming Commission, gaming taxes and fees amounted to more than $327 million in fiscal 2002. That's $73 million more than the corporate taxes paid by all other industries combined, making it the state's third-largest source of revenue, second only to sales tax and income tax. In addition, the Mississippi gaming industry has provided more than sixteen thousand direct jobs with a payroll of more than $240 million. It's estimated that gaming provides another $140 million in sales, income, alcoholic beverage, room, and property taxes. Prior to the arrival of gaming, the leading industry on the Mississippi Gulf Coast was shrimping—not exactly a huge growth business.

With all this good fiscal news for a smaller market state like Mississippi, there's plenty of food for thought for other states across the country that haven't already jumped on the gaming bandwagon. And yet, there's still a good deal of old-school thinking, archaic laws, and outright hypocrisy holding back the industry's growth. The industry in Mississippi, as well as in other states, is being held back by the bible-thumping zealots of the Deep South and the Bible Belt. At the same time, these casinos are bankrolling the state budget.

States have sometimes thrown up impediments making it difficult for the gaming industry. For instance, by law all Mississippi casinos must be located above water, which means that they must be located either along the Gulf Coast, on or over the Mississippi River, or on riverboats. Other states allow gaming only on riverboats, which doesn't make a whole lot of sense. While attending the gaming convention I stayed at the huge, multimillion-dollar Beau Rivage, owned by MGM Mirage, and frankly, I couldn't even tell that I was over water. This is a five-star, four-diamond, permanent hotel and believe me, whether built on the water or over it, it's not going anywhere.

The number one topic of the conference's first day was making the casinos land-based. I think that if gaming is allowed anywhere in the state, or in the United States for that matter, it should be legal everywhere, near water or not, and taxed accordingly, which means not onerously. Nevada, which obviously knows the power of gaming revenue, taxes it at an average of only 7.5 percent. At the other end of the spectrum, Illinois taxes gaming revenue with a new top bracket of a whopping 70 percent! Obviously, Illinois politicians foolishly think they can allow gaming and then, because they consider it socially irresponsible, tax it to the hilt. As a result, it should come as no surprise that gaming operators are rethinking growth prospects in

Illinois and their commitment to that state, as compared to more hospitable venues.

A Brief History of Gaming

Gambling has existed in various forms for thousands of years. The first written references to gambling date back to around 2300 B.C. in China. The citizens of ancient Greece also were known to wager their valuables in games of chance, while Romans notoriously entertained themselves by betting on chariot races and the grisly outcomes of matches between gladiators.

Dice games have been popular for more than two thousand years and turn up in chronicles of ancient Rome and China. The roots of the modern-day game of craps lie in the old English game of hazard, which reaches back to at least the fourteenth century and was played for high stakes in English gaming rooms. After the French adopted the game, a roll of two ones, or "snake-eyes," as it became known, was nicknamed "crabs," which later was transformed into "craps." As Europeans settled in the Americas, a simplified version of the game developed and took hold throughout the old south and western frontier. Today, craps is one of the top-revenue attractions in U.S. casinos, ranking only behind the slot machines and blackjack.

Today's card games are also thought to have come down to us from the Chinese. Around A.D. 900, the Chinese apparently came up with the idea by shuffling early paper money into a variety of combinations. English and French adventurers brought card games to the New World in the fifteenth and sixteenth centuries. The contemporary fifty-two card deck was invented sometime in the 1600s and was originally referred to as the "French Pack." This pack was taken up by the English and later became popular in America. "Poque," the forerunner of modern-day poker, flourished in French New Orleans. Blackjack originated in French casinos around 1700 and has been played in the United States since the 1800s. In the late 1950s and the 1960s, mathematicians began to study the game closely and provided gamblers with systematic ways in which to play nearly even with the house—or perhaps even gain a slight edge. This scientific approach helped to make blackjack the number one table game in the United States in the 1960s and it has remained so to the present day.

For centuries, lotteries have been used to fund public works such as roads and buildings, and even to finance wars. Scholars have come up with conflicting theories about the ancient origins of the practice, but there are even references to lotteries in the Old Testament. Moses, after all, used a kind of lottery to award land west of the River Jordan. Funds raised by lottery games are believed to have been used to finance construction of the Great Wall of China, and medieval European villagers gathered in the town square to cast their lots as a form of entertainment. In more recent times, lotteries were used to fund the Virginia Company and America's first English settlement at Jamestown. All thirteen original colonies turned to lotteries to raise revenue. In the 1700s, Benjamin Franklin, George Washington, and John Hancock endorsed the idea of using lotteries for public works projects; in fact, Ben Franklin's lottery financed the purchase of cannons for the Revolutionary War. In a more peaceful vein, lottery proceeds were used to establish some of the nation's oldest universities, including Harvard, Yale, Columbia, and Princeton. Years later, growing unhappiness with tax increases led to the establishment of modern state-sponsored lotteries of the twentieth century. New Hampshire was the first state to run its own lottery in 1964. New York and New Jersey followed closely behind—in 1967 and 1971. During the next five years, an additional thirteen states opened lotteries, and by 1990 a majority of states were in the lottery business.

Most people associate gaming in the United States with Las Vegas. In 1931, hoping that the completion of Boulder Dam would bring hordes of tourists to Nevada, the state legalized most forms of gambling. Ironically, although illegal gambling had thrived in Nevada for years, the legal casino gambling industry did not catch on at first. Only after World War II, when the country entered a new era of prosperity, did the casino business take off. In 1941, El Rancho was opened as the first large resort on Las Vegas's famous "Strip." Mobster Bugsy Siegel opened the Flamingo Hotel in December 1946 and helped make Las Vegas, rather than Reno, the top casino destination for Hollywood stars and other high rollers.

Legalized gambling was confined to Nevada until 1978, when New Jersey followed suit, seeking to bring new life to the seedy resort area of Atlantic City. But it was in the 1990s that the idea really caught on nationally. Since 1989, casinos have popped up in almost twenty states as gambling gained acceptance and state governments acknowledged the benefits of gaming revenues.

Since the Pequot Tribe opened Foxwoods in Connecticut, the first casino on Indian property in 1992, casinos on Indian reservations have thrived. As Timothy L. O'Brien points out, "The Pequots originally intended to keep Foxwoods open only eighteen hours a day. But the casino stayed open around the clock from the moment its doors opened, and the Pequots have never looked back . . . by 1996, forty-five thousand people *per day* were visiting Foxwoods."

As a result of the success of Foxwoods, dozens of other casinos have sprung up on reservations across the country, but all of them are, of course, privately owned. A number of publicly traded companies, however, can build, manage, and supply machines to the Native American reservation casino business.

Investing in Vice

Industry Performance

Most of the stocks of the gaming and casino industry have had phenomenal returns over the past six years. The MUTUALS.com study completed in July 2002 and updated in July 2003 compared the gaming and casino industry as a whole to the Standard & Poor's 500 Index. Although many market researchers have gaming stocks in one industry and hotels that are casinos in another, we combined hotel casinos with gaming stocks to complete the analysis.

From June 30, 2002, through June 30, 2003, gaming and casinos gained 24.65 percent, while the Standard & Poor's 500 Index lost 1.55 percent. The three-year total return (not annualized) for gaming and casinos was a nice 68.36 percent while the S&P 500 lost 33.01 percent. The five-year total showed a 145.13 percent gain, while the S&P 500 still had a 14.05 percent loss from June 1998 through 2003.

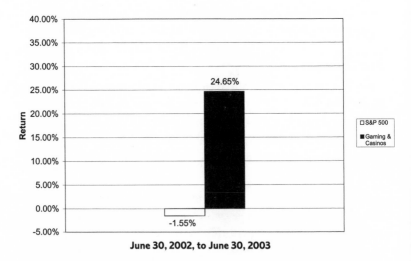

Figure 4.1. One-year return, gaming and casinos versus S&P 500 Index.

Gaming: Place Your Bets

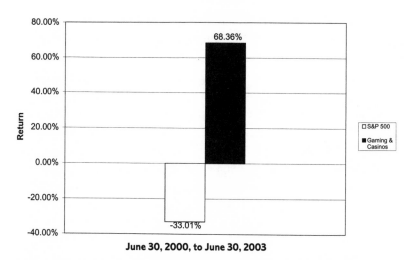

Figure 4.2. Three-year return, gaming and casinos versus S&P 500 Index.

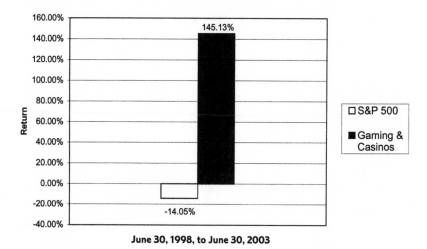

Figure 4.3. Five-year return, gaming and casinos versus S&P 500 Index.

In each of the industry studies conducted by MUTUALS.com, we used the same methodology. We included all of the industry's U.S. publicly traded stocks plus foreign firms traded on the U.S.

market. The stocks were market-cap weighted, as are most market indexes such as the Standard & Poor's 500 Index. As explained earlier, market capitalization is simply the market price of the entire company. It's calculated by multiplying the number of shares outstanding by the price per share. A company with a $1 billion market capitalization counts toward the index ten times as much as a $100 million company. To simplify the analysis, all firms with less than $50 million of market cap were eliminated, since the small companies are statistically insignificant. A list of gaming and casino companies used in the study follows in Figure 4.4. In the next section, I'll discuss favorite stocks in detail.

Top Gaming Stocks

HARRAH'S ENTERTAINMENT (HET)

Harrah's Entertainment, Inc., began operations in the casino business in 1937 and was incorporated in the fall of 1989. The company, conducting business through a wholly owned subsidiary called Harrah's Operating Company, Inc. (HOC) now operates approximately twenty-six casinos in fourteen states, although those numbers change often.

By the beginning of 2003, Harrah's Entertainment owned or operated more than 1.5 million square feet of casino space, 42,000 slot machines, 1,000 table games, 14,000 hotel rooms or suites, over 350,000 square feet of convention space, and 100 restaurants.

The company-owned casinos include:

- Harrah's Atlantic City

- The Mardi Gras–themed Atlantic City Showboat in New Jersey

Company (Ticker)	Market Capitalization
International Game Tech. (IGT)	$8.8 billion
MGM Mirage (MGG)	$5.3 billion
Harrah's Entertainment, Inc. (HET)	$4.4 billion
Park Place Entertainment (PPE)	$2.6 billion
Mandalay Resort Group (MBG)	$1.9 billion
Station Casinos, Inc. (STN)	$1.5 billion
Wynn Resorts, Ltd. (WYNN)	$1.4 billion
Boyd Gaming Corp. (BYD)	$1.1 billion
Alliance Gaming Corp. (AGI)	$1.0 billion
Kerzner International Lim (KZL)	$897.5 million
Penn National Gaming, Inc (PENN)	$824.6 million
Argosy Gaming Company (AGY)	$623.2 million
Ameristar Casinos, Inc. (ASCA)	$578.0 million
Aztar Corp. (AZR)	$559.9 million
Scientific Games Corp. (SGMS)	$533.9 million
Magna Entertainment Corp. (MECA)	$530.4 million
Churchill Downs, Inc. (CHDN)	$507.3 million
Shuffle Master, Inc. (SHFL)	$498.9 million
Isle of Capri Casinos (ISLE)	$495.8 million
WMS Industires, Inc. (WMS)	$473.5 million
Multimedia Games, Inc. (MGAM)	$324.3 million
Dover Downs Gaming & Ente (DDE)	$255.5 million
MTR Gaming Group, Inc. (MNTG)	$218.8 million
Pinnacle Entertainment (PNK)	$182.1 million
Nevada Gold & Casinos (UWN)	$95.1 million
Monarch Casino & Resort (MCRI)	$88.9 million
Youbet.com, Inc. (UBET)	$88.7 million
Lakes Entertainment, Inc. (LACO)	$88.3 million
Mikohn Gaming Corp. (MIKN)	$77.2 million
Interlott Technologies (ILI)	$57.6 million

Figure 4.4.

Investing in Vice

- Harrah's Las Vegas and Rio All-Suite Hotel and Casino in Nevada

- Harrah's Vicksbury in Mississippi

- Harvey's Harrah's in Joliet, Illinois

- Harrah's Lake Tahoe

- Harrah's Shreveport in Louisiana

- Harvey's Resort and Casino and Bill's Casino in Lake Tahoe, Nevada

- Harrah's Reno in Reno, Nevada

- Harrah's Laughlin in Nevada

- Harrah's East Chicago Casino and Hotel in Indiana

- Harrah's Tunica, a dockside casino in Mississippi

- Harrah's New Orleans, a casino in Louisiana

- Harrah's North Kansas City in Missouri

- Harrah's St. Louis in Missouri

- Harrah's Metropolis in Illinois

- Harrah's Council Bluffs in Iowa

- Harrah's Lake Charles in Louisiana

Gaming: Place Your Bets

Harrah's Entertainment also manages a number of casinos, including:

- Harrah's Rincon Casino and Resort in Southern California

- Harrah's Phoenix Ak-Chin casino in Arizona

- Harrah's Cherokee Smoky Mountains Casino in North Carolina

- Harrah's Prairie Band Casino-Topeka in Kansas

Some other Harrah's holdings include:

- Harrah's manages a greyhound track in Council Bluffs, Iowa, and owns an interest in Turfway Park, in Kentucky

- Bluffs Run Casino, a dog-racing facility located in Council Bluffs, Iowa

- Bluegrass Downs, a harness racetrack located in Paducah, Kentucky (the track holds live racing meets each fall, as well as year-round simulcasting of horse racing events)

Thoughts

Compared to other competitors, Harrah's has done a great job with regional expansion. This means that the company is not overly susceptible to drop-offs in tourism as it would be in single-destination spots such as Atlantic City and Las Vegas. And yet Harrah's maintains a major presence on the Vegas Strip, Atlantic City, and at least twelve other states. In addition, it is involved in the management of some of the Native American casinos.

Another strong asset for Harrah's is its Total Rewards program, which is widely regarded as the best player-loyalty program in the nation, with an enormous database of more than twenty-five million names.

We also believe that Harrah's has a great brand name and a very focused business model, especially as compared to its primary Las Vegas competitor, Park Place, which, despite owning some large, profitable properties seems to have a disjointed, unfocused business mission.

Throughout the financial downturn between 2000 and 2003, Harrah's has continued to have strong revenue growth, operating margin expansion, and free cash flow. As with many gaming stocks, I believe Harrah's can continue substantial growth and even with its phenomenal stock performance can still be viewed as undervalued at current prices.

MULTIMEDIA GAMES (MGAM)

Incorporated on August 30, 1991, Multimedia Games, Inc., supplies interactive electronic games and electronic player stations to the Native American gaming market. MGAM delivers the electronic games to its customers through Betnet, a telecommunications system that allows players to compete against one another in the same game to win prizes.

Multimedia Games also develops all the design systems—software, content, and networks—for its casino customers.

It offers high-speed, interactive bingo games including Mega-

Mania, Big Cash Bingo, Flash 21 Bingo, and People's Choice, plus a new generation of games called MegaNanza and Reel Time Bingo.

In May 2002, MGAM was selected to provide the central operating system for New York's video lottery system.

Thoughts

Multimedia Games, which is the primary supplier of gaming machines to the Native American community, can offer an investor exposure to a smaller cap, potentially faster-moving stock (of course, along with this goes greater risk). MGAM is an attractive investment because it offers great exposure to the profitable and growing Native American casino industry, which is otherwise not available as a direct investment. This is important because Standard & Poor's estimates that gaming revenues at Native American facilities now total about 30 percent of the industry totals. During the next several years, new casinos on Native American land in California, New York, and other areas of the country are likely to be a significant source of growth.

SHUFFLE MASTER (SHFL)

Incorporated in 1983, Shuffle Master, Inc., designs, produces, and markets a number of technology-based products for the gaming industry. Its primary business, as the name would imply, is automatic card shufflers. As of the beginning of 2003, almost ten thousand of its shufflers were installed in gaming establishments around the world. The shufflers are sold under several trademarks, including Shuffle Master Gaming, ACE, King, MD, and Deck Mate. SHFL's Shufflers are automatic card shuffling machines designed for use with multideck table games in casinos and other legal gaming businesses. The automatic shufflers provide enhanced security and greater productivity by limiting possible card manipulation by dealers and speeding up games. One recent innovation by the company is the development of the Deck Mate, a single-deck/double-deck card shuffler for use on single- or double-deck blackjack tables and poker tables.

Table games produced by Shuffle Master include Let It Ride, Let It Ride Bonus game, and the Three Card Poker game. Shuffle Master also develops and markets slot games such as The Three Stooges, Spider-Man, Let's Make A Deal, Hollywood, The Honeymooners, Press Your Luck, and Five Deck Poker games.

In the summer of 2002, Shuffle Master acquired the technology, patent, and products of Casino Software Services, LLC and began marketing Bloodhound, formerly known as Blackjack Survey Voice, to its customers around the world. Bloodhound is used by casinos to rate and track the play of blackjack customers. During fiscal 2002, the company also developed several new table games, including Crazy 4 Poker and Triple Shot Bonus.

Thoughts

I like Shuffle Master because it provides us with quality exposure to the latest gaming technology. As a supplier of automatic card shufflers that speed up card games and therefore speed up per-table revenue, the product is obviously very attractive to casinos.

As casinos continue to be built around the country, Shuffle Master is a corporation that can profit through each expansion because of the machines and technology it supplies. The company also has exposure to the booming slot industry, but in my opinion is not being overpriced, as is its huge competitor, International Game Technology (IGT).

GTECH HOLDINGS CORPORATION (GTK)

GTECH Corporation, a wholly owned subsidiary of GTECH Holdings Corporation, is a global information technology company that operates lottery transaction processing systems for—or supplies equipment and services to—almost two thirds of the thirty-nine online lottery authorities in the United States. It also operates or services online lottery systems for more than half of the 105 international online lottery authorities.

GTECH provides lottery technology services of every kind, including the design, assembly, installation, operation, maintenance, and marketing of online lottery systems. GTECH's offerings include central computer systems, systems software, and game software, as well as the hookups to retail-store lottery terminals.

A critical element in GTECH's strategy is to design new products and develop services that will help lottery authorities to generate increased revenues. Among these new product lines are instant ticket support systems and Keno, an online lottery game that offers drawings as often as every five minutes. GTECH is also involved in televised lottery programs such as Bingo Vision.

Thoughts

Although not included on the list of all gaming and casino companies, I consider GTECH and the lottery business to be an important part of the gaming industry. As explained earlier, the lottery industry is booming and we see no end in sight. The few states that do not yet have lotteries (or whose lotteries are limited) are beginning to think they are missing out on the action and seem to be moving toward either expansion or introduction. Furthermore, those states with established lottery programs have grown accustomed to the lottery revenues and certainly won't scale back their lottery programs, but will only look to expand.

GTECH is a dominant player, with state and national lotteries on six continents. With very few competitors in the industry, it has what many investors call a wide economic moat. GTECH has not only been able to grow, but has been able to increase market share regularly.

KERZNER INTERNATIONAL LIMITED (KZL)

Kerzner was formerly known as Sun International Hotels, Ltd. It's a developer and operator of casino resorts and luxury hotels in a number of premier destinations. The company owns and operates the Atlantis Paradise Island resort and casino in the Bahamas and developed the huge Mohegan Sun Casino in Uncasville, Connecticut. The Mohegan Sun is Native American–owned but still supplies income to Kerzner. The company also operates eight beach resorts at locations in Mauritius, Dubai, the Maldives, and the Bahamas (owning nearly 70 percent of Paradise Island.)

The Bahamas

Atlantis, its flagship property, is a 2,317-room, ocean-themed casino resort, with three interconnected hotel towers (the Royal

Tower, the Coral Tower and the Beach Tower) built around a seven-acre lagoon and a thirty-four-acre marine environment that includes an open-air aquarium. Atlantis also boasts a huge entertainment complex offering approximately one thousand slot machines and eighty table games, seventeen restaurants, one hundred thousand square feet of convention space, a sports center, more than thirty thousand square feet of luxury retail space, and a full service marina with sixty-three slips.

Kerzner also owns and operates the 106-room Ocean Club Resort, a high-end luxury resort hotel located on Paradise Island, plus the Ocean Club Golf Course, a water plant, and other improvements on Paradise Island.

Connecticut

Mohegan Sun, which incorporates its historical Native American theme throughout the resort, is one of the most profitable casinos in the United States. It is one of only two casinos in an area servicing approximately 22 million adults (Foxwoods Resort is the other). The casino contains approximately 296,000 square feet of gaming space, featuring more than 6,200 slot machines, 240 table games, and forty-two poker tables. Connecticut is actually the fourth largest gaming market in the United States

Atlantic City

In the spring of 2001, Kerzner sold Resorts Atlantic City. However, the company still owns approximately thirteen acres of valuable land adjacent to Resorts Atlantic City, which is available for development.

Indian Ocean Resorts

Kerzner manages and owns interests in five Indian Ocean beach resorts, including the 175-room Le Saint Geran Hotel, the 200-room Le Touessrok Hotel & Ile Aux Cerfs, the 248-room La Pirogue Hotel, the 333-room Le CoCo Beach, and the 238-room Sugar Beach Resort Hotel.

Dubai

Kerzner manages the Royal Mirage Hotel, a luxury 258-room hotel on Jumeira Beach, which was constructed to resemble an Arabian fortress. Royal Mirage's rooms account for more than 10 percent of the total rooms on the popular beach.

Maldives

Kerzner manages and has 25 percent ownership interest in Kanuhura, a luxurious, 120-room resort located on Kanuhura Island in the Maldives, approximately six hundred miles southwest of the southern tip of India.

Other Interests

Sun International Resorts, Inc., Kerzner's indirect wholly owned subsidiary, provides support services, marketing services, travel reservations, and wholesale tour services for the Paradise Island operation. Through another wholly owned subsidiary, Kerzner owns a tour operator company in France called Sun

Vacances that offers planning and reservation services for travel to many of Kerzner's properties around the world.

Thoughts

Kerzner is a great company that's unknown to many individual investors despite its fairly large market capitalization. It does, however, own the huge, well-known Bahamas Atlantis property, which the company is in the process of expanding. Kerzner provides great diversification from the U.S. gaming and casino industry. Its incredible worldwide real estate holdings alone provide a great deal of book value for the stock.

5

Tobacco: Smoke 'Em if You Got 'Em

If I cannot smoke in heaven, then I shall not go.

—Mark Twain

In recent years, most investors have tracked the U.S. stock market by looking at the Standard & Poor's 500, NASDAQ, and the Dow Jones Industrial Average. In the late 1960s and early 1970s, long before the explosion of mutual funds and online brokerage, many investors watched what was known as the "Nifty Fifty," which comprised fifty large, blue chip, well-known companies that included Johnson & Johnson, General Electric, Coca-Cola, Walt Disney, McDonald's, IBM, Kodak, Merck, and most of the thirty stocks that make up the Dow Jones Industrials. The consensus of the day was that "you couldn't go wrong" by investing in a mix of these fifty solid companies.

Today, very few investors can predict what the top stock performer of any sector, industry, or other grouping will be. But if you had to guess which one stock has outperformed such "great" stocks as GE, Coke, McDonald's, Merck, Disney, Johnson & Johnson, and all the others in the Nifty Fifty over the past thirty years (including dividends) which one would it be?

I'd guess that very few if any would have said Philip Morris (MO), now called Altria, but in fact, that's the right answer. Only a few relatively new names on the market, like Wal-Mart, Home Depot, Intel, and Microsoft have outperformed MO since 1970. But they certainly weren't members of the well-known Nifty Fifty back in the 1970s.

Tobacco may be one of my "vice" groups, but it is also an industry that is extremely important to the world's economy. Tobacco contributes substantially to the economy of more than 150 countries and is responsible for the employment of more than 100 million people worldwide. In fact, tobacco is the world's most widely cultivated nonfood crop and is responsible for more employment per hectare of cultivated land than any other crop in the world. Despite the fact that less than 0.3 percent of the world's agricultural land is used for tobacco farming, farmers are able to earn healthy yields from small plots of tobacco, which in some cases enables them to put these earnings back into growing other crops. And tobacco is also an important source of tax revenue for almost every government in the world.

As a significant U.S. crop, the U.S. Department of Agriculture (USDA) provides financial assistance to tobacco producers through a complex system of price supports, nonrecourse loans, crop insurance, research services, and even direct payments. First established in 1933, the tobacco program stabilizes prices above normal market prices. The U.S. government is using taxpayer dollars to subsidize the production of a product that they are taxing to the hilt as a sin stock once it is produced. I doubt that the government will ever let the tobacco tax income stream come to an end.

Tobacco: Smoke 'Em if You Got 'Em

A similar situation exists in Europe, where the European Union spends almost 1 billion euros a year on tobacco subsidies. This compares to the 11.5 million euros that the E.U. spent each year on the Europe Against Cancer campaign until it ended in 2000. Of course, Europe Against Cancer received more press because it was "politically correct."

Socially responsible investors probably feel that they should boycott the stock of large tobacco companies like Altria (Philip Morris) because they're in the business of selling cigarettes and other tobacco products. To avoid being hypocrites, however, these people should probably boycott all Altria products, shouldn't they? But what's the likelihood of that happening?

As of December 31, 2002, Altria owned approximately 84.2 percent of the outstanding shares of Kraft's capital stock through its ownership of 50.2 percent of Kraft's class A common stock and 100 percent of Kraft's class B common stock. As of December 31, 2002, the company held approximately 98 percent of the combined voting power of Kraft's outstanding capital stock. On December 11, 2000, Kraft acquired all of the outstanding shares of Nabisco Holdings Corp. Few people realize all the products under the umbrella of Kraft and Nabisco. I don't think many so-called socially responsible investors are prepared to avoid Oreo, Chips Ahoy!, Snack Wells, Ritz, Premium, Triscuit, Wheat Thins, Cheese Nips, Planters, Life Savers, Jell-O, Maxwell House, General Foods International Coffees, Capri Sun, Tang, Kool-Aid, Crystal Light, Kraft cheese, Kraft macaroni and cheese, Philadelphia cream cheese, Velveeta, Cheez Whiz, Cool Whip, Post cereals, Cream of Wheat, A1 steak sauce, Bull's-Eye, Grey Poupon, Shake 'N Bake, Milk-Bone, DiGiorno, Tombstone, Lunchables, Oscar Mayer, Louis Rich, and Stove Top Stuffing.

The truth is, the situation is a lot more complicated than these socially responsible investors would have us believe, in part, because Altria is such a diversified company.

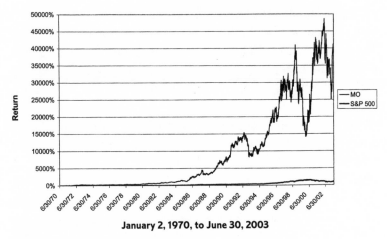

January 2, 1970, to June 30, 2003

Figure 5.1. Performance of Altria (Philip Morris), January 1970 to June 2003, versus S&P 500 Index.

Take a look at the above chart and you will get an idea of the tremendous growth Philip Morris (Altria) has undergone over the last three decades. This is a truly amazing feat for a company that much of the U.S. public mistakenly just thinks of as "bad."

Today, the U.S. tobacco industry is one of the most profitable business in the country, and it remains this way despite years of legal battles, increased government regulations and declining rates of consumption. Also, according to Standard & Poor's, the operating margins for U.S. tobacco companies are in the 30 percent range, well above that of the companies that sell packaged foods and alcoholic beverages.

The Dangers of Tobacco

Many investors shy away from investing in the tobacco industry because they fear both government regulations and the threats of legal action. However, in an ironic twist, it seems that government regulation of the tobacco business has actually helped make the industry more profitable. How? Well, for one thing, when the government banned the tobacco companies from advertising on television in 1971, it resulted in decreased marketing costs without any discernible loss of revenue. Massive tobacco tax increases also provide a built-in mechanism for increases in operating margin. When a state or city government, for example, hits tobacco with a new twenty-cent per pack tax increase, it's simple for the manufacturer to slip in a new one- or two-cent price increase to increase their profit margin. The result? Cash-rich tobacco companies.

Tobacco stocks pay some of the highest dividends on the market. The U.S. government has decided to help us out in this area too. As part of President George W. Bush's new tax plan, dividend taxes will be greatly reduced starting in 2003. I won't go into details, since at the time of this writing, the plan still isn't finalized, but dividends from domestic corporations, mutual funds, and some foreign corporations will see a great deal of tax relief. Tobacco stockholders, as well as dividend-paying alcohol and defense stockholders, should benefit greatly. We'll benefit in two ways: dividend income at reduced tax rates and indirect gains in stock prices. As soon as the tax package is put in place, high-dividend-paying stocks could see a good boost due to simple supply and demand. Many investors may move money from non-dividend-paying stocks, bonds, and money markets to the big-dividend payers such as Altria and R. J. Reynolds, so they can enjoy the tax-favored income these stocks provide.

As for legal actions, certainly they pose a threat to profits, but in spring 2003 a Florida appeals court overturned a landmark $145 billion judgment against major U.S. tobacco companies and ordered the enormous class action decertified. In making the ruling in the so-called Engle class action, the Florida

Third District Court of Appeal said, "The proceedings that produced the findings of entitlement and the $145 billion award were irretrievably tainted by class counsel's misconduct and the award is bankrupting under Florida law."

And remember, these legal actions are in large part unique to the United States and therefore do not substantially affect the business these companies conduct overseas.

Even though the U.S. tobacco market may be shrinking somewhat, the industry has not been sitting on its hands, bemoaning the possible loss of revenue. Instead, the large tobacco companies, like Altria, have cast their gaze well beyond our shores in search of the growth that they might be missing here. They have been successful, in part due to rising incomes in many developing countries, high per capita cigarette consumption, and an increasing taste for American-style cigarettes (thanks to their high flue-cured tobacco content). As an example of simple responses to obvious problems in the United States, Philip Morris International announced in early 2003 that it would increase cigarette output in Russia from 40 billion cigarettes a year to 70 billion by 2005—a 75 percent increase! Most of the major cigarette manufacturers are following suit with their international production.

Overall, the tobacco industry has adapted well to a set of circumstances that, at least on paper, don't seem to be all that conducive to a successful business. But then, historically, tobacco always has had its ups and downs.

A Brief History of Tobacco

By the beginning of the first century A.D., tobacco was well-known in the Americas and was often used in religious ceremonies. The first pictorial record of smoking was found on a pottery vessel that dates somewhere before the eleventh century. It depicts a Maya smoking a roll of tobacco leaves tied with a string.

When Columbus made his voyage to the New World, he was introduced to tobacco, as evidenced by entries in his journal in which he wrote, "[T]he natives brought fruit, wooden spears, and certain dried leaves which gave off a distinct fragrance." Later, he wrote, "We found a man in a canoe going from Santa Maria to Fernandia. He had with him some dried leaves which are in high value among them, for a quantity of it was brought to me at San Salvador."

In 1600, Sir Walter Raleigh persuaded Queen Elizabeth to take up smoking and twelve years later, John Rolfe and his wife Rebecca, more widely known as Pocahontas, raised Virginia's first commercial crop of "tall tobacco."

By the seventeenth century, tobacco had gained a strong foothold in the country, even so far as being used as currency in the colonies. "Country Money," or "Country Pay," was used as a monetary standard. As an odd little sidelight, in 1619, when the first shipment of women meant to become wives for the settlers arrived in Jamestown, a prospective husband was expected to pay for his chosen mate's passage with 120 pounds of tobacco. At one time, the western part of what is now Greenwich Village in New York City was known to the Native Americans there as Sapponckanican—"tobacco fields," or "land where the tobacco grows." And in France, Napoleon was said to have used seven pounds of snuff tobacco each month.

In 1760, Pierre Lorillard established a plant in New York City for processing pipe tobacco and snuff, making P. Lorillard the oldest tobacco company in the United States. Two years later, General Israel Putnam introduced cigar smoking to the United

States when, after a British campaign in Cuba, the general returned with three donkey loads of Havana cigars.

The founding fathers were not immune to the lure of tobacco. For some time, tobacco was George Washington's main cash crop, which he sold in England and Continental Europe. Eventually, Washington and other tobacco growers grew weary of dealing with the extra fees imposed by England as well as the fluctuating tobacco prices. As a result, especially in the area known as the "Tobacco Coast," along the Chesapeake River, the Revolutionary War was actually known as "The Tobacco War." In fact, tobacco helped finance the Revolution by serving as collateral—five million pounds of Virginia tobacco—for the loan Benjamin Franklin managed to get from France. Washington himself, in need of support for the army, appealed to the colonists, "If you can't send money, send tobacco." During the war, tobacco exports helped fund the rebellion and once the victory over England was complete, many states levied tobacco taxes to help repay the Revolutionary War debt. In 1794, Congress passed the first federal 8 percent excise tax on snuff, which was opposed by James Madison who argued that it deprived poorer Americans of one of life's simpler gratifications.

During the Civil War, both the North and the South gave out tobacco with rations, and in 1862, a new federal tax on tobacco was instituted to help pay for the Civil War—it yielded close to $3 million. Two years later, the first American cigarette factory opened, producing nearly twenty million cigarettes that first year.

Many of us associate the connection between tobacco and health as a relatively new revelation, but in truth, this is not the case. In 1674, for instance, Russia banned smoking for health reasons and the punishment for breaking this ban was the death penalty. Fortunately for the Russian citizens who enjoyed a good smoke every now and then, this ban was lifted just two years later. In 1683, Massachusetts passed the nation's first no-smoking law, forbidding the smoking of tobacco outdoors, because of the danger of fire. Not long after, Philadelphia approved a ban on "smoking seegars on the street," and the fines that were collected were used to purchase firefighting equipment.

In 1868, the British Parliament passed a Railway Bill that mandated smoke-free cars to prevent injury to nonsmokers. Twenty-five years later, Washington banned the sale and use of cigarettes in the state. In 1898, the Tennessee Supreme Court upheld a total ban on cigarettes, ruling that they were "not legitimate articles of commerce, because wholly noxious and deleterious to health, their use is always harmful." This link between cigarettes and health was furthered by Dr. Isaac Adler who, in a 1912 monograph, was the first person to strongly suggest that lung cancer was related to smoking. A year later, the American Society for the Control of Cancer, later to be known as the American Cancer Society, was formed.

And yet, the use of cigarettes and other tobacco products somehow managed to grow in popularity. For instance, when cigarettes were rationed during World War I, those who were opposed to shipping cigarettes to solders were accused of being traitors. As General John J. Pershing said, "You ask me what we need to win this war. I answer tobacco as much as bullets. Tobacco is as indispensable as the daily ration; we must have thousands of tons without delay." The War Department responded by purchasing the entire output of Bull Durham tobacco, resulting in the Bull Durham ad, "When our boys light up, the Huns will light out." During the war in Iraq in 2003, the U.S. and British troops were at it again. They were seen on CNN passing out cartons of smokes to the Iraqi citizens along with food and water.

In 1922, however, fifteen states still banned the sale, manufacture, possession, advertising, and use of cigarettes. But this prohibition against tobacco didn't last long after the boost from World War I, and a mere five years later, Kansas became the last state to drop its ban on cigarette sales.

Today, many local governments have once again declared war on cigarette smokers, either by levying enormous taxes or by outlawing smoking in public places, or both. As a result, the tobacco industry has a huge problem with public perception. Philip Morris has been vilified in the press to the extent that most investors don't even realize that the stock has outperformed the Standard & Poor's 500 Index by a good margin for the past three years.

Performance

The performance of Philip Morris, or Altria, is indicative of the entire tobacco industry. Most investors simply don't know that the industry as a whole has performed as well as it has. In fact, tobacco has returned a whopping 107.57 percent gain over the past three years (more than doubling) versus the Standard & Poor's 500 Index loss of 33.01 percent. From June 30, 1998, through June 30, 2003, the tobacco industry as a whole has gained 56.70 percent, while the S&P 500 Index has lost 14.05 percent for that period. Over the most recent year, June 2002 through June 2003, tobacco had a tough time with some serious ups and downs in the crazy U.S. court systems. Stocks of the tobacco industry still showed a total one-year gain of 10.40 percent compared to the S&P 500 loss if 1.55 percent.

Tobacco companies as a group have continued to pay out some of the best dividends in the U.S. market.

The returns mentioned above include all of the tobacco industry's U.S. publicly traded stocks plus foreign firms traded on the

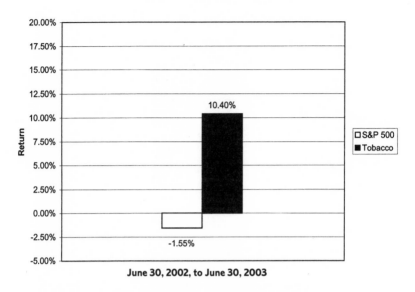

Tobacco: Smoke 'Em if You Got 'Em

June 30, 2002, to June 30, 2003

Figure 5.2. One-year return, tobacco versus S&P 500 Index.

U.S. market. The stocks were market-cap weighted, like the Standard & Poor's 500 Index. All firms with less than $50 million of market capitalization were eliminated, due to statistical insignificance. A list of tobacco companies used in the study follows at the end of the chapter in Figure 5.5.

Top Tobacco Stocks

ALTRIA GROUP (MO)

Formerly known as Philip Morris Companies, Inc., Altria Group, Inc., is a holding company and the parent to a number of famous subsidiaries. Altria includes Philip Morris USA, Inc., Philip Morris International, Inc., and its majority-owned subsidiary,

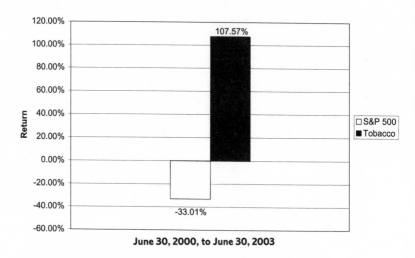

Figure 5.3. Three-year return, tobacco versus S&P 500 Index.

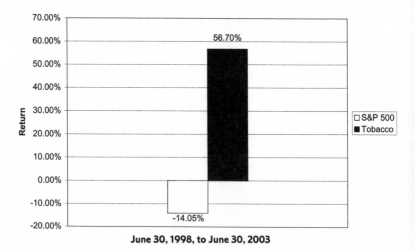

Figure 5.4. Five-year return, tobacco versus S&P 500 Index.

Kraft Foods, Inc. (Kraft). Altria subsidiaries are engaged in the manufacture and sale of various consumer products, including cigarettes, foods, and beverages.

The company changed its name from Philip Morris Companies, Inc. to Altria Group Inc. in January 2003. Philip Morris USA is engaged in the production and sale of cigarettes, its most popular brand worldwide being Marlboro, one of the world's most recognized brands.

Kraft manufactures and sells food and beverage products in the United States, Canada, Europe, the Middle East, Africa, Latin America, and the Asia Pacific region. Kraft conducts its global business through its subsidiaries: Kraft Foods North America, Inc., and Kraft Foods International, Inc. It sells products in more than 150 countries and has operations in more than sixty countries. As of December 31, 2002, Altria owned approximately 84.2 percent of the outstanding shares of Kraft's capital stock.

Tobacco Products

Philip Morris USA manufactures, markets, and sells cigarettes in the United States and exports American tobacco products overseas. The company's major brands are Marlboro, Virginia Slims, and Parliament. Philip Morris International's leading brands include Marlboro, L&M, Philip Morris, Bond Street, Chesterfield, Virginia Slims, Merit, Parliament, and Lark.

Food Products

Kraft has recently expanded its market through the December 2000 acquisition of Nabisco Holdings Corporation (Nabisco). Subsequently, Kraft Foods International purchased a snack business in Turkey, a biscuit business in Australia, confectionery businesses in Russia and Poland, and coffee businesses in Romania, Morocco, and Bulgaria.

Kraft Foods North America principal brands include Oreo, Chips Ahoy!, Newtons, Nilla, Nutter Butter, Stella D'Oro, and Snack Wells cookies; Ritz, Premium, Triscuit, Wheat Thins, Cheese Nips, Better Cheddars, Honey Maid Grahams, and Teddy Grahams crackers; Planters nuts and salted snacks; Life Savers, Creme Savers, Altoids, Gummi Savers, and Fruit Snacks; Terry's and Toblerone chocolate, Jell-O refrigerated gelatin and pudding snacks; and Handi-Snacks pudding. Kraft also owns Balance Bar Company and Boca Burger, Inc.

Beverage products produced by the company include Maxwell House, General Foods International Coffees, Starbucks, Yuban, Sanka, and Gevalia coffees; Tang, Kool-Aid, and Crystal Light aseptic juice drinks, and Kool-Aid, Tang, Crystal Light, and Country Time powdered beverages. Cheese products include Kraft and Cracker Barrel natural cheeses, Philadelphia cream cheese, Kraft and Velveeta process cheeses, Kraft grated cheeses, Cheez Whiz process cheese sauce, Easy Cheese aerosol cheese spread, and Breakstone's cottage cheese and sour cream.

In what they call the convenience meals sector, brands include DiGiorno, Tombstone, Jack's, California Pizza Kitchen, and Delissio frozen pizzas; Kraft macaroni and cheese dinners; Taco Bell, Stove Top Oven Classics meal kits; Lunchables lunch combinations; Oscar Mayer and Louis Rich cold cuts, hot dogs, and bacon; Boca soy-based meat alternatives; Stove Top stuffing mix, and Minute Rice.

Major grocery brands include Jell-O dry packaged desserts; Cool Whip frozen whipped topping; Post ready-to-eat cereals; Cream of Wheat and Cream of Rice hot cereals; Kraft and Miracle Whip spoonable dressings; Kraft salad dressings; A1 steak sauce;

Kraft and Bull's-Eye barbecue sauces; Grey Poupon premium mustards; Shake 'N Bake coatings, and Milk-Bone pet snacks.

Financial Services

Philip Morris Capital Corporation, another wholly owned subsidiary, is primarily engaged in leasing activities, including aircraft, electrical power, real estate, surface transportation, manufacturing, and energy industries. By the end of 2002, total assets of Philip Morris Capital were over 9 billion dollars.

Thoughts

As I mentioned in the previous alcohol chapter, due to huge economies of scale and barriers to entry, the tobacco business is controlled by only a handful of companies. Philip Morris *is* the tobacco industry. As it goes, so goes the rest of the industry. The company has done a great job of choosing its battles and using its legal resources wisely. It has top legal counsel and so far has won most court fights. The press only tells us about the major setbacks, or when those setbacks are overturned. When legal judgments become too obtrusive, Philip Morris has actually called in support from other States' Attorneys General, who need to support their "cash cow." When tax increases hit, the company raises prices to assure a good profit. When domestic tobacco consumption slumps, it increases internationally. Despite obvious threats from multibillion-dollar lawsuits and judgments, I think Altria has built-in profits and protections for years to come and is a great bargain at the stock prices witnessed in 2002 and 2003.

Through Kraft and Nabisco, Altria owns a truly amazing group of brand names. I like to list the full pool of brands since they are used in virtually every household in America. Altria is not going away, as much of the press would have you believe.

IMPERIAL TOBACCO GROUP ADR (ITY)

Incorporated in 1996, Imperial Tobacco Group PLC produces and markets a wide range of tobacco and tobacco-related products. Cigarette brands include Embassy, Regal, Superkings, John Player Special, Lambert & Butler, Richmond, Horizon, The Imperial, West, Davidoff, R1, Prima and Cabinet. Roll-your-own tobacco brands include Drum, Golden Virginia, Van Nelle, and Interval. ITY also offers Classic cigars, Amphora and St. Bruno pipe tobacco, and Rizla rolling papers.

Imperial Tobacco products are sold in more than one hundred countries and duty-free markets, particularly in the United Kingdom, Germany, The Netherlands, Belgium, Ireland, Australia, France, Hungary, Ukraine, Russia, Poland, Slovakia, Taiwan, and Kyrgyzstan.

Imperial is targeting growth in a number of emerging markets in southeast Asia, with new operations in Vietnam. In 2002, the company acquired a controlling interest in the state-owned manufacturer and distributor of cigarettes in Laos.

In the United Kingdom, the company owns Lambert & Butler, an old British cigarette brand family. The company also distributes the Marlboro brands in the United Kingdom for Philip Morris. In connection with its recent acquisition of more than 90 percent of the German cigarette manufacturer Reemtsma Cigarettenfabriken GmbH, ITY relaunched the famous Davidoff cigarette brand, and it is now their most internationally distributed brand. Until recently Davidoff had been only available in a few international hotels and select locations in central London.

The company does a significant amount of tobacco product distribution in Germany, France, and Spain. In Central Europe, the company distributes its brands in Poland, Slovenia, Hungary, Macedonia, the Czech Republic, and Slovakia as well as Ukraine, Russia, and Kyrgyzstan.

In the Middle East, the Davidoff brand is available in several Persian Gulf markets including Saudi Arabia and Kuwait. The company enhanced its presence in Africa after acquiring Tobaccor, S.A., in March 2001.

Thoughts

Few investors in the United States realize the huge worldwide tobacco market and the fact that most of the tobacco industry's legal and regulatory problems are confined to the United States. Imperial Tobacco is a worldwide leader. It is one of the world's five largest tobacco companies and dominates outside the United States. Imperial is a FT-SE 100 company listed on the London Stock Exchange, but it's also listed on the New York Stock Exchange as an ADR (American depository receipt). As an ADR, it's readily available to U.S. investors but simply not well known. One of the greatest growth strengths of Imperial Tobacco comes from its Davidoff brand, as top brand names continue to expand worldwide and replace smaller, regional brand names. Imperial is at the forefront of growth in developing areas like Eastern Europe, Southeast Asia, and Africa, and Davidoff should lead the way.

BRITISH AMERICAN TOBACCO ADR (BTI)

Established over one hundred years ago, British American Tobacco is the world's second largest public tobacco group. It is an international cigarette manufacturer with manufacturing and processing operations around the world. Their products are distributed to millions of retail establishments throughout the world, including supermarkets, hotels, restaurants, cafes, tobacconists, and duty-free shops.

Their international brands include Dunhill, Lucky Strike, Kent, State Express 555, Rothmans, Peter Stuyvesant, Benson & Hedges, Kool, Pall Mall, Viceroy, Winfield, and John Player Gold Leaf. Their local brands include Jockey Club (Argentina), Stradbroke (Australia), du Maurier (Canada), North State (Finland), HB (Germany), Sopianae (Hungary), Wills (India), Ardath (Indonesia), Carrolls (Ireland), Boots (Mexico), Jan III Sobieski (Poland), Yava Gold (Russia), Courtleigh (South Africa), Parisienne (Switzerland), GPC (United States), and Xon (Uzbekistan).

The company also manufactures cigars, fine-cut tobacco, and pipe tobacco. The company's most well known cigar brands are Mercator, Dunhill, and Schimmelpenninck. Their fine-cut brands are famous in Europe and include Samson, Ajja, Javaanse Jongens, and locally favored brands such as Schwarzer Krauser in Germany. Their leading pipe tobacco brands include Clan, Erinmore, Captain Black, and Dunhill.

Thoughts

British American Tobacco likes to say that it is the world's most international tobacco group. Its brands are sold in more than 180 markets around the world, so it provides even more developing market growth potential than Imperial Tobacco. Like

Imperial Tobacco, I like British American for the worldwide dominance that leads to good predictable cash flow and great dividends, without most of the legal problems associated with tobacco in the United States. Also, like Imperial, BTI's stock is traded as an ADR, which is "off the radar screen" of many investors.

UST, INC. (UST)

UST, Inc., incorporated in 1986, produces and markets smokeless tobacco products as well as several wine brands. They used to go by the name US Tobacco, until tobacco turned into such a distasteful word in the United States. The company also has international operations, involving smokeless tobacco products and premium cigars.

UST's moist tobacco brands are Copenhagen, Skoal Long Cut, Skoal Copenhagen Long Cut, Red Seal, Skoal Bandits, and Rooster. Its dry tobacco brands are Bruton, CC, and Red Seal. In 2002, the company began offering three new premium products: Skoal Long Cut Berry Blend, Copenhagen Pouches, and Skoal Wintergreen Pouches. The company's cigar brands include Don Tomas, Astral, and Helix.

UST harvests grapes from its own vineyards, although it also depends on grapes purchased from independent growers in Washington and California. UST's wines are marketed throughout the United States and include Chateau Ste. Michelle, Columbia Crest, Villa Mt. Eden, and Conn Creek. It also produces Domaine Ste. Michelle sparkling wine.

Investing in Vice

Thoughts

A U.S.-based tobacco company without smoker's lawsuits? What's not to like? And, like other tobacco companies, UST pays great dividends. (A handful of lawsuits by smokeless tobacco users have been reported.)

SWEDISH MATCH A.B. (SWMAY)

Swedish Match A.B., headquartered in Stockholm, is an international company that is involved in niche tobacco products, including cigars, snuff, pipe tobacco, chewing tobacco, matches, and lighters. The company has almost 15,000 employees, and production facilities in fifteen countries. It markets products in more than 140 countries worldwide.

Swedish Match's business goal is to become a unique tobacco company by getting its extremely popular niche tobacco products to gain acceptance in growing markets in line with current social and consumer trends.

In mid-2001, Swedish Match acquired the smokeless tobacco trademarks of Premium Tobacco Traders, Ltd. This acquisition allowed the company to market dry snuff products in Germany, Switzerland, and France.

Cigars

Swedish Match sells cigars in nearly one hundred countries and owns over twenty famous cigar brands. In North America, as a result of the company's 64 percent acquisition of General Cigar Holdings, Inc., Swedish Match offers premium cigar brands such as Partagas, Punch, Hoyo de Monterrey, Cohiba, and Macanudo. In Europe Swedish Match offers both handmade and machine-made cigars. Its largest machine-made brand is La Paz, a big seller in Europe. Under the La Paz brand label, Swedish Match offers tube-encased cigars as well as super coronas and panatelas.

Snuff

Swedish Match produces snuff products for the American, Northern European, and South African markets. In North America, snuff is sold in both a premium and a value segment. Brands include Timber Wolf and Renegades portion-packed snuff. European brands include Goteborgs Rape, Ettan, General, Catch and Grovsnus. In South Africa, Swedish Match markets its snuff under a brand called Taxi.

Chewing Tobacco

In North America, Swedish Match's primary brand is Red Man, marketed in both traditional and the milder Golden Blend. Since most of the U.S. market is in the southeast, the company has recently developed a new brand called "Southern Pride."

Pipe Tobacco

Swedish Match sells pipe tobacco in North America, Western Europe, and South Africa. The company's primary brands include Borkum Riff, Mellow Breeze, Half and Half, Velvet, and Paladin. In South Africa, the company sells pipe tobacco under the Boxer brand, which is also distributed in Mozambique and Namibia.

Matches

The company sells its matches primarily in Western Europe, Brazil, Indonesia, and India. Under the brand names of Solstickan, Redheads, and Bryant & May, the company has also introduced several other products in Western Europe, such as grill firelighters and fire logs.

Lighters

Swedish Match also sells disposable lighters—including the famous Cricket brand—in Europe, parts of Asia, and the United States. The company has also introduced an electronic pocketlighter. Other brands in this category include Feudor and Poppel.

Thoughts

Swedish Match is a well-diversified company and, as a result, it's immune to much of the U.S. tobacco industry problems. As UST dominates the United States smokeless tobacco market, Swedish Match owns the European snuff market. In Sweden, more people actually use snuff than smoke cigarettes. Snuff use is a trend that's beginning to spread into much of Europe. I feel that Swedish Match has great upside potential as smokeless tobacco is promoted as a "safer" alternative to cigarette smoking.

Tobacco: Smoke 'Em if You Got 'Em

Company (Ticker)	Market Capitalization
Altria Group, Inc. (MO)	$93.4 billion
British American Tobacco (BTI)	$24.1 billion
Imperial Tobacco Group, PLC (ITY)	$13.1 billion
Gallaher Group, PLC (ADR) (GLH)	$6.4 billion
UST, Inc. (UST)	$6.1 billion
R. J. Reynolds Tobacco (RJR)	$3.1 billion
Swedish Match A.B. (ADR) (SWMAY)	$2.5 billion
Universal Corp. (UVV)	$1.1 billion
Loews Corp. Carolina Group (CG)	$1.1 billion
Vector Group, Ltd. (VGR)	$658.3 million
DIMON, Inc. (DMN)	$318.5 million
Standard Commercial Corp. (STW)	$230.7 million
Star Scientific, Inc. (STSI)	$182.7 million

Figure 5.5. List of tobacco companies with market capitalization.

6

Defense: Bombs Away

*A good plan, violently executed now, is better than a
perfect plan next week.*

—General George S. Patton Jr.

In a perfect world, George S. Patton would not
have been a general; he might have been the CEO of General
Motors. In a perfect world, we wouldn't need companies like
General Dynamics, Lockheed Martin, and Northrop Grumman
to produce tanks, warplanes, ships, and missiles.

Unfortunately, we don't live in a perfect world. We live in a
world that has been at war since the beginning of recorded history. There doesn't seem much chance of this changing any time
soon. Is there a moment of any day where there isn't an armed
conflict going on somewhere in the world? Of course not. And
the tragic and disturbing events of the last two years have certainly shown Americans that we are not immune to conflict even
within our own borders. Defense means just that—preparing to

defend yourself, not simply creating weapons to invade, conquer, and destroy other nations.

Ten years ago, the geopolitical environment was far more stable than it is today. Sure, we were able to handle Iraq, but at the time of the writing of this book there are indications that al Qaeda terrorists still pose a threat; North Korea remains a destabilizing influence; India and Pakistan are still at the brink of a confrontation; and the Middle East is a spark away from bursting into a full-blown conflagration.

For this reason, I don't see the U.S. government lowering its allocations for defense anytime soon. In fact, the Bush administration currently projects spending on defense to climb to $450 billion by 2007, up considerably from the $370 billion spent today. Additionally, consider that during the peak of the Cold War, we spent about 10 percent of our gross domestic product on defense versus the less than 4 percent we spend today.

Also, because of the changing nature of war, defense money is spent on a lot more than tanks and planes and ships and ammunition. Today, much of the defense budget is spent on homeland defense, which includes communications, bomb-detection devices, and other high-tech expenditures.

Some of the socially responsible investors would have us believe that all weapons manufacturers should be avoided. I disagree. The aerospace and defense industries employ hundreds of thousands of American citizens and adds billions to the U.S. economy. Eliminating defense stocks from a portfolio also means eliminating all aerospace companies, along with all their technological innovations in air travel, space exploration, communications, energy research and development, and a multitude of material and method applications that carry over to our daily lives. For instance, because warfare strategies have changed so dramatically over the past two decades, the use of satellite technology has grown enormously, as it is used in battlefield communications, tracking, reconnaissance, and weapons guidance. This certainly means that there will be growth in the satellite sector. Also, I believe the defense and aerospace industries could power the next tech boom, without many of the risks of the last tech boom, which was led by the private sector and the effects of which we're still experiencing.

One of the world's largest corporations, General Electric (GE), is shunned by many of the socially responsible "police," because it is one of the world's leading suppliers of military jet engines. I guess GE doesn't get any "brownie points" for its cutting-edge technology in fighting heart disease, or innovations in alternative energy—wind turbine, hydroelectric, and hydrogen fuel cell.

Defense firm United Technologies Corporation (UTX), which provides the military with Pratt & Whitney engines and Sikorsky helicopters, also owns Carrier Corporation. Carrier was the first air-conditioning company to shut down the manufacture of equipment using ozone-damaging CFCs. Since the 1980s, Carrier has spent more than $100 million to design CFC usage out of equipment worldwide. Also, United Technologies' fuel cell business is among the pioneers in the field of pollution-free fuel cell research and development. But, once again, the so-called socially responsible view UTX as only an evil defense contractor.

Lockheed Martin (LMT), like GE and United Technologies, is a leader in innovative research and development, but the company also serves as an example of great diversity in employment practices. In the first part of 2003, it was:

- Ranked "Number One place for Women to Work" by *Woman Engineer Magazine*

Investing in Vice

- Voted number one by readers of *Minority Engineering Magazine* in "Top 50 Companies"

- Ranked thirteen by the readers of *Career & the disAbled* in "Top 50 Companies"

Are they a socially irresponsible company? I don't think so.

Whether you like it or not, the defense industry in this country is an enormous business. According to the weekly publication *Defense News,* which covers the global military sector, the 100 largest global defense contractors in 2001 generated somewhere in the neighborhood of $180.6 billion in revenues. I see that number increasing at a respectable pace in the coming years.

In the early- to mid-1990s, the U.S. defense industry became more consolidated. Today, although there may be more than 100 defense-related companies worldwide, the bulk of the business is conducted by only a handful of top companies such as Lockheed Martin Corporation (LMT), the Boeing Company (BA), Northrop Grumman Corporation (NOC), Raytheon (RTN), General Dynamics Corporation (GD), the United Kingdom's BAE Systems, and European Aeronautic Defense & Space Company (Europe's largest aerospace firm).

According to figures provided by the Teal Group, which is an independent aerospace research and consulting firm, the U.S. military accounts for more than 40 percent of the total defense weapons market. Europe accounts for 24 percent, the Middle East 20 percent, Latin America 4 percent, and Africa 4 percent. U.S. defense firms are obviously the leading suppliers to the worldwide aerospace/defense market.

Defense: Bombs Away

Performance

Over the past five years, the aerospace and defense industries have performed very well, but probably not in the time period the average investor would imagine. Going to war does not make defense stock prices shoot upward. Historically, defense stocks have often performed very well following the resolution of conflict, but not during conflict. For the one-year period of June 30, 2002, through June 30, 2003, defense stocks as a group returned −23.62 percent, while the Standard & Poor's 500 Index lost 1.55 percent. On the other hand, a bad year for defense isn't "technology bad," to use a term I mentioned in chapter 1. Over the longer time period, however, defense stocks showed stronger returns while the overall market lost money. For three years, the aerospace and defense industries rose 22.71 percent total (not annualized), while the S&P 500 lost 33.01 percent. Over the June 1998 through June 2003 five-year period, defense dropped only 6.59 percent total, while the S&P had a total return of −14.05 percent.

As in previous chapters, the above study includes all of the aerospace and defense industries' U.S. publicly traded stocks and any foreign firms traded on the U.S. market. The stocks were market-cap weighted, like the Standard & Poor's 500 Index. All firms with less than $50 million of market capitalization were eliminated, due to statistical insignificance. A list of defense contractors used in the study follows near the end of the chapter in Figure 6.4.

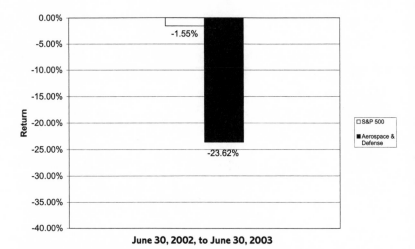

Figure 6.1. One-year return, aerospace and defense versus the S&P 500 Index.

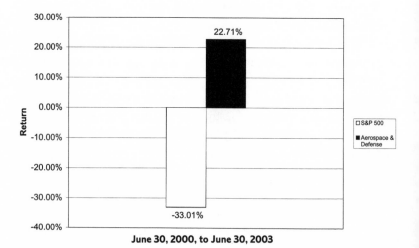

Figure 6.2. Three-year return, defense and aerospace versus S&P 500 Index.

Defense: Bombs Away

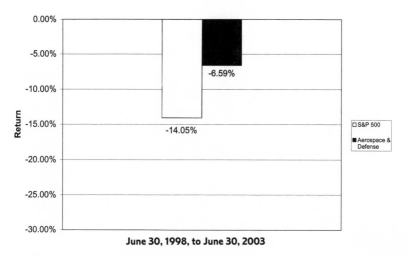

Figure 6.3. Five-year return, defense and aerospace versus S&P 500 Index.

Top Defense and Aerospace Stocks

L-3 COMMUNICATIONS (LLL)

Organized in 1997, L-3 Communications Holdings, Inc. (L-3 Holdings) develops and provides communications and intelligence, surveillance and reconnaissance systems, simulation services, and aircraft modernization.

The company's primary markets include the United States Department of Defense; United States government intelligence agencies; other federal, state, and local government agencies; and some foreign governments. It also works with aerospace and defense contractors, and other commercial customers.

L-3 has completed numerous key mergers and acquisitions. In March 2002, the company acquired Integration Systems, a division of Raytheon Company, and renamed it L-3 Communications Integrated Systems. In November 2002, L-3 Holdings purchased

Westwood Corporation, a company focused on shipboard power control, switchgear and power distribution systems. In December 2002, L-3 acquired Ship Analytics, Inc., in the homeland security arena. It produces management software for command and control in homeland security applications. In March 2003, L-3 Holdings Avionics Systems, previously a division of Goodrich Corporation and a producer of general aviation safety systems.

Finally, in early 2002, L-3 acquired two firms: Spar Aerospace Limited and SY Technology, Inc., which specialize in air warfare simulation; command, control, communications, computers, and intelligence; plus missile defense and space systems technology.

L-3 Communications is comprised of several different segments. Among them are:

- Training, Simulation & Support Services—offering a wide range of training and simulation services. It provides training for aircrews, navigators, mission operators, gunners, and maintenance technicians for various military aircraft and ground vehicles. They also provide simulation tools used by the Department of Defense, Department of Homeland Security and U.S. government intelligence agencies that involve missile and space systems and unmanned aerial vehicles.

- Secure Communications & ISR—offering products and services for the global intelligence, surveillance, and reconnaissance (ISR) market. It specializes in signals intelligence and communications intelligence systems. They provide secure, high-data-rate communications systems for reconnaissance and surveillance applications needed by the U.S. military as well as by foreign governments.

- Aviation Products & Aircraft Modernization—offering aviation products and aircraft modernization services such as airborne traffic and collision avoidance systems for commercial and military aircraft. It provides commercial crash-protected cockpit voice recorders, flight data recorders, and maritime voyage recorders. It also produces custom displays for military and high-end commercial applications.

Thoughts

L-3 Communications is thought of by some as a technology company and by others as a defense contractor. In reality, it's a tech company that has the benefit of catering almost entirely to U.S. and foreign governments, intelligence agencies, and major aerospace and defense contractors. If there is to be another tech boom driven more by the public sector, L-3 will be on the cutting edge. Since defense contracts last for many years, even decades, L-3 Communications has a great deal of growth potential, without many of the risks connected to private sector technology firms.

NORTHROP GRUMMAN CORPORATION (NOC)

In May 1994 the Northrop Corporation was renamed Northrop Grumman Corporation, following the purchase of Grumman Corporation. Since then, they've made fifteen acquisitions concluding with December 2002's $10.7 billion deal to acquire TRW and their satellite business.

Northrop's seven business sectors include:

Investing in Vice

Electronic Systems

Electronic Systems designs, develops, and produces a wide range of defense electronics including airborne radar systems, secondary surveillance systems, inertial navigation systems and sensors, electronic warfare systems, precision weapons, air traffic control systems, air defense systems communications systems, space systems, and marine systems. Its products are used in the F-16 fighter, F-22 fighter, new F-35 joint strike fighter, Apache helicopter, AWACS radar, Hellfire missile, and numerous other systems.

Information Technology

The company's Information Technology segment is divided into: Government Information Technology; Enterprise Information Technology; Technology Services; and Commercial Information Technology. These businesses cover a wide range of large-scale systems integration, networks, hardware, software, communications, intelligence, surveillance and reconnaissance, training and simulation, science and technology, and enterprise-wide infrastructure.

Integrated Systems

Integrated Systems develops and manufactures airborne early warning, electronic warfare, surveillance, and battlefield management systems. Integrated Systems has a major role in the F/A-18 Hornet strike fighter and F-35 joint strike fighter programs, and is the main contractor for the B-2 stealth bomber.

Defense: Bombs Away

Newport News Shipbuilding

Newport News's principal business is the design, construction, repair, maintenance, and refueling of nuclear-powered aircraft carriers and nuclear-powered submarines for the United States Navy.

Mission Systems

Mission Systems provides global system integration services for complex, mission-enabling systems. Services involve strategic missiles, missile and air defense, airborne reconnaissance, unmanned aerial vehicles, and electromagnetic and infrared analysis.

Ship Systems

Ship Systems is a full-service provider for the design, engineering, construction, and support of major surface ships for the U.S. Navy, the Coast Guard, and numerous international navies. It also works with commercial vessels of all types.

Space Technology

The company's Space Technology segment focuses on the design and manufacture of spacecraft systems, high-energy laser systems, solar arrays and reflectors, communication systems for space and defense, commercial telecommunications products, and other scientific instruments for use in space.

Thoughts

I could fill page after page with all the reasons why Northrop Grumman Corporation was named the Forbes 2003 Company of the Year. It is an extremely well-managed company, with good financials, and a well-defined business model and growth strategy.

NOC management has pieced together a diverse group of leading-edge capabilities and technologies that, when combined with its system integration strategy, places the company directly in line with the U.S. government's vision of the future. As an example, Eric McDonald, my portfolio co-manager, loves to boast that with TRW's satellite systems, Northrop now has a laser that can actually shoot a bullet out of the sky.

With its TRW acquisition, NOC is now the second largest U.S. defense contractor in terms of revenue and the largest federal IT services provider. As the federal government's largest IT provider, I see practically locked-in revenue for years to come.

LOCKHEED MARTIN CORPORATION (LMT)

The principal business of Lockheed Martin Corporation is researching, designing, and manufacturing advanced flight systems and products. It's most famous for producing jet fighter warplanes. The company serves customers in domestic and international defense, civil, and commercial markets, but their primary customer is the U.S. government. In 2002, approximately 80 percent of the company's net sales were made to the United States. The company operates in business segments that include Aeronautics, Space Systems, Systems Integration, and Technology Services.

Defense: Bombs Away

Aeronautics

The Aeronautics segment focuses on the design, research and development, production, and support of advanced military aircraft. Customers include the major military branches of the United States and allied countries around the world. Major programs and products include the F-16 multirole fighter, F/A-22 strike fighter, F-35 Joint Strike Fighter, and C-130 and C-5 airlifts. They are also involved in support of the F-117 Stealth and multiple reconnaissance aircraft including the U-2.

Space Systems

The company's Space Systems division designs, engineers, and produces numerous commercial and military space systems. Many of its systems are used for intelligence, surveillance, and reconnaissance. As of the end of 2002, the Space Systems Division's net sales represented about 28 percent of the company's total sales.

Systems Integration

The company's Systems Integration division designs and manufactures a number of systems for undersea, shipboard, land, and airborne uses. With the Systems Integration unit, Lockheed is involved in homeland security, radar, air traffic control systems, avionics to ground combat vehicle integration, surveillance and reconnaissance systems, and communications, computers and intelligence systems for naval, air, and ground personnel. It also produces missiles, ship and submarine combat systems, and antisubmarine and undersea warfare systems.

Technology Services

Lockheed's Technology Services division provides a wide assortment of information management, engineering, scientific, and logistic services to numerous federal agencies and some commercial customers. Technology Services is another area of Lockheed that's involved in homeland security. Primary customers include the Department of Defense and the National Aeronautics and Space Administration (NASA).

In June 2003, Lockheed Martin acquired the ORINCON Corporation International. It operates primarily in the intelligence, surveillance, and reconnaissance (ISR) industry and will add to Lockheed's share of the intelligence market.

Thoughts

Through Lockheed Martin's great long-term jet fighter contracts worldwide, the firm has a revenue stream for decades to come. Because of these contacts, LMT has among the lowest downside earning surprise risk as compared to its big-capitalization defense peers. As an industry leader with a niche in the jet fighter market, the stock should be owned by investors seeking defense sector exposure in today's market. Defense stocks in general are undervalued based on historical prices as well as the solid outlook for the industry.

UNITED DEFENSE INDUSTRIES (UDI)

Incorporated in 1997, United Defense is an industry leader in the design, development, and manufacture of combat vehicles, artillery, naval guns, missile launchers, and precision munitions. UDI's customers include the U.S. Department of Defense and numerous allied governments. The company focuses on research and development in key technologies, including the development of combat system operating software. The company also provides nonnuclear ship repair, modernization, and conversion services to the U.S. Navy and related agencies.

In 2002, the company acquired United States Marine Repair, Inc., whose principal client is the United States Navy. It provides ship repair and modernization services to all types of nonnuclear vessels. USMR also performs ship repair services for other U.S. departments and agencies, as well as some commercial customers.

The Defense Systems segment of the company is the prime contractor for the Bradley Fighting Vehicle and has added numerous technology-based upgrades to the Bradley Fighting Vehicle. It has also developed several new manned ground vehicles in the Army's Future Combat Systems program, including the Non-Line-of-Sight Cannon.

United Defense also has a joint venture located in Turkey called FNSS Savunma Sistemleri A.S., which pursues armored combat vehicle sales to the Turkish Army, and it has been involved in a joint venture in Saudi Arabia providing modernization services.

Thoughts

UDI is a very interesting company. It is a smaller capitalization stock in an industry of very large and old companies like General Dynamics and Northrop Grumman. While most defense companies are moving their business toward high-tech aerospace, United Defense is there to handle the combat vehicles, artillery, naval guns, missile launchers, and munitions, along with ship repair and modernization. Somebody has to do it.

UDI has good earnings, but the stock is available at a very attractive price/earnings ratio as compared to the majority of the aerospace and defense industries.

MANTECH INTERNATIONAL CORPORATION (MANT)

Founded in 1968 and incorporated in 1998, ManTech International Corporation offers a wide range of information technology and technical services to the U.S. government. As of 2002, the company derives approximately 85 percent of its revenues from defense programs for the Department of Defense and various intelligence agencies.

ManTech operates in three primary areas: IT Solutions, Systems Engineering Solutions, and Secure Systems and Infrastructure Solutions.

IT Solutions

ManTech provides systems integration services and network maintenance services to its government customers. ManTech also analyzes information systems, applications, and platforms, and it develops solutions to extend systems performance and availability. It provides e-commerce and Web development for numerous government agencies. ManTech offers a wide range of services that manage information for its customers by performing comprehensive systems administration and support for mission operations.

Defense: Bombs Away

Systems Engineering Solutions

In this area, ManTech provides services that analyze customer hardware and software needs and performs tests in the certification of new systems. Areas include acoustics, vibration, and electromagnetic tests and are used in aircraft, shop, submarine, and space applications. ManTech tests ordinance effectiveness and stealth capabilities.

Secure Systems and Infrastructure Solutions

ManTech provides a wide range of services that enhance systems and network availability for the Department of Defense and intelligence agencies. ManTech provides secrecy and security infrastructure services for classified programs including intelligence operations and military programs, and it provides for safeguarding of numerous secure communication systems.

ManTech provides services that identify potential foreign and domestic threats, including terrorism, and recommends countermeasures. Capabilities include adversary characterization, threat modeling, vulnerability identification, security assessment, physical countermeasures, cyber countermeasures, and disaster recovery assessment.

In late 2002, ManTech acquired CTX Corporation, a provider of information technology and software to the national intelligence community. In early 2003, ManTech acquired Integrated Data Systems. It develops systems integration services and software for national intelligence agencies and the Department of Defense. In the spring of 2003, ManTech acquired MSM Security Services, Inc., which supplies personnel investigation services to the United States government.

Company (Ticker)	Market Capitalization
Boeing Company (BA)	$27.7 billion
Honeywell International (HON)	$23.3 billion
Lockheed Martin Corp. (LMT)	$21.8 billion
Northrop Grumman Corp. (NOC)	$15.7 billion
General Dynamics Corp. (GD)	$14.3 billion
Rockwell Collins, Inc. (COL)	$4.5 billion
Embraer-Empresa Brasileir (ERJ)	$3.0 billion
Goodrich Corp. (GR)	$2.5 billion
Alliant Techsystems, Inc. (ATK)	$2.0 billion
Precision Castparts Corp. (PCP)	$1.7 billion
United Defense Industries (UDI)	$1.4 billion
FLIR Systems, Inc. (FLIR)	$1.1 billion
Elbit Systems, Ltd. (ESLT)	$748.9 million
Curtiss-Wright Corp. (CW)	$664.5 million
DRS Technologies, Inc. (DRS)	$633.2 million
Triumph Group. Inc. (TGI)	$451.6 million
Esterline Technologies (ESL)	$376.8 million
EDO Corporation (EDO)	$353.4 million
Orbital Sciences Corp. (ORB)	$341.4 million
Integrated Defense Technologies (IDE)	$337.0 million
Kaman Corp. (KAMNA)	$253.0 million
HEICO Corp. (HEI)	$252.2 million
Herley Industries, Inc. (HRLY)	$237.3 million
Aviall, Inc. (AVL)	$230.5 million
AAR Corp. (AIR)	$223.3 million
United Industrial Corp. (UIC)	$213.1 million
Ducommun Inc. (DCO)	$137.3 million
Metal Storm, Ltd. (ADR) (MTSX)	$122.0 million
BE Aerospace, Inc. (BEAV)	$115.4 million
Fairchild Corp. (FA)	$104.0 million
Allied Defense Group (ADG)	$103.2 million
Pemco Aviation Group, Inc. (PAGI)	$95.3 million
Innovative Solutions & Su (ISSC)	$89.8 million
Sensytech, Inc. (STST)	$89.3 million

Figure 6.4. List of defense and aerospace stocks and market capitalization.

Defense: Bombs Away

Thoughts

ManTech, in a situation similar to that of GTECH in the gaming chapter, is not officially listed as a defense stock. It's not, for instance, part of the group in Figure 6.4. Instead, ManTech is listed in the technology sector and software and programming industry. We, of course, know that it's a defense contractor—the U.S. government is its primary customer—and I love its technology-based growth potential. It's a small cap, five-year-old company, which is in exactly the right place at the right time to fit the needs of intelligence agencies and the Department of Defense.

7

Sex: Where's the Porn?

*Sex is one of the most wholesome, beautiful, and
natural experiences that money can buy.*

—Steve Martin

No matter what state the economy is in, one
thing remains constant: Sex sells.

When you consider pay-per-view cable, adult videos, sexually
oriented magazines, subscription Web sites, and a multitude of
other products, the sex industry generates billions of dollars
annually. Perhaps a sign that the sex industry is here to stay, as if
anyone needed one, The Daily Planet, a brothel in Melbourne,
Australia, went public this spring.

But the crucial question is, does the sex industry make for a
viable investment? Generally speaking, the answer is no. Most of
the money in the sex industry is being made either directly by
private companies, not publicly traded stocks, or indirectly by
major corporations whose primary business is something else.
Most of the publicly traded companies whose primary business

line is "adult entertainment" are small, poorly funded, thinly traded penny stocks. Billions of dollars are being made in pornography, but it's not flowing into these stocks.

In terms of the portfolio, I don't hold any sex industry stocks in our investments at the present time—in other words, I don't invest in pornography, gentleman's clubs, legal prostitution, or other areas of adult entertainment. But this is a totally pragmatic decision, not because of any judgmental, holier-than-thou, finger-pointing moralism. I simply haven't found any large, legal, growth-oriented companies in this industry worth investing in.

In this chapter, I'll list and discuss the companies in the sex industry that are publicly traded, and take a look at some non-public stocks that are profiting in the business of porn.

Publicly Traded Sex Stocks

CHURCH & DWIGHT

Church & Dwight, through its stake in Armkel (a 2001 joint venture with the private equity group, Kelso & Company), owns 50 percent of the Trojan condom business: Trojans are America's top-selling brand of condoms. The company, based in Princeton, New Jersey, was founded in 1846 as a producer and seller of baking soda. They're still very much in the baking soda business, marketing a variety of bicarbonate-based products under the familiar label of Arm & Hammer. At the same time, the company has taken an aggressive and innovative approach to marketing the Trojan brand, promoting sales in part by emphasizing sexual pleasure rather than safety. Indeed, one of their newest products, Trojan Extended Pleasure, has quickly become one of the industry's biggest sellers.

Sex: Where's the Porn?

The problem with investing in Trojan is that it is much too small a part of Church & Dwight's overall business—condom sales provide hardly more than an estimated 5 percent of the company's earnings—to have much of an effect on their bottom line. Thus, if you purchased Church & Dwight stock, you wouldn't be doing it on the basis of the sales of Trojan.

NEW FRONTIER MEDIA (NOOF)

New Frontier Media distributes pornography, primarily video, and is reported to control about 25 percent of the U.S. market. In 2002, it had $52 million in reported revenue and owned six sexually explicit television networks. Growth seems possible with the expansion of satellite and digital cable, but New Frontier is simply too small an operation to make for a viable investment in our portfolio. As of spring 2003, its market capitalization was around $20 million, and with a stock price below $2.00, less than $50,000 worth of stock traded on an average daily basis. NOOF is a very high-risk penny stock that is of no interest to me.

PRIVATE MEDIA GROUP (PRVT)

Based in Barcelona, Spain, Private Media Group purchases movies and photographs for use in magazines, videotapes, and DVDs. The company also published the world's first legal hard-core sex magazine, *Private,* which is distributed in more than thirty-five countries. In addition, it finances more than 100 movies each year and boasts the world's biggest porn library. North America only accounts for 34 percent of its sales. As with most other sex industry investments, Private Media, whose June

2003 market cap is only $80 million, is simply too lightly traded to make it a wise investment. PRVT stock also happens to have lost more than 66 percent in 2002 and was down more than 40 percent through June of 2003. I wouldn't call it a value stock. I'd simply call it a lousy investment.

RICK'S CABARET INTERNATIONAL (RICK)

Rick's Cabaret International is the first publicly traded topless bar chain. It also features an adult membership Web site business, which offers a number of Internet auction sites such as NaughtyBids.com, which sells items such as clothes worn in porno films. In 2002, Rick's, which employs more than four hundred people, generated $15.5 million in revenue but showed a net loss in income. Once again, it is too small a company to make for a good investment. RICK has a tiny market cap and is very lightly traded with about three thousand shares changing hands on average each day. You simply can't buy a reasonable number of shares on the open market without greatly changing the price to your disadvantage.

PLAYBOY ENTERPRISES (PLA)

Playboy Enterprises is the granddaddy of the sex industry. *Playboy* magazine, founded by Hugh Hefner in the early 1950s, has a readership of 4.5 million. The company also has pay-per-view television, home videos, cable, and product merchandising. Playboy is the biggest and most prestigious player in the adult entertainment market, yet for the past two years its sales have been flat due in part to the drop in its publishing business.

Lately, however, due to increased growth in cable and pay

Sex: Where's the Porn?

TV, the company has significantly improved the bottom line. I think Playboy is a well-run company. It's actively traded and widely owned by companies including Fidelity, Vanguard, Janus, and Putnam. The problem is that it's not really growth oriented. Growing shareholder value simply isn't a primary concern of the company. Its primary concern is entertainment, and it does it well. Even Hugh Hefner has said that he wished that he'd never taken the stock public since he now has to answer to two bosses—the magazine's readers and the company's shareholders.

BEATE UHSE AG (USE, on the German exchange)

Beate Uhse is an interesting stock traded in Europe, but not readily available in the United States. The company runs Europe's largest mail-order erotic business, plus more than 100 Beate Uhse sex shops in Austria, Belgium, Italy, the Netherlands, Norway, Spain, and Switzerland. Its operations include wholesale and manufacturing, plus a huge Internet porn network. To top off its porn empire it runs the Museum of Erotica in Berlin—not exactly a "family" destination like Walt Disney World or Universal Studios. Leave the kids at home.

Privately Owned Sex Companies

Some significant privately owned companies in the business of sex include Vivid Entertainment; LFP, Inc.; and General Media, Inc.

- Vivid is the world's top producer of adult films, releasing approximately eighty new titles each year.

Investing in Vice

- LFP stands for Larry Flynt Productions, famous for *Hustler* magazine and First Amendment court battles. The company actually distributes more than thirty magazine titles.

- General Media, Inc., publishes *Penthouse* magazine and a few other periodicals. General Media is owned almost entirely by Penthouse International, which in turn is 85 percent owned by Bob Guccione, the founder.

If any of these companies go public some day, I may have to reconsider the lack of porn in my investments. But for now, I'll be sticking with mostly alcohol, tobacco, gaming, and defense stocks.

8

Investing in Vice

He that is without sin among you, let him cast the first stone.

—John 8:7

Now that I've laid out the basic reasons for investing in vice, including some individual stocks I like in each industry, I'd like to review the various ways to invest, including mutual funds, discount brokerage firms, and full-service firms. I'll also discuss some pros and cons of each method, along with some doctrines of successful investing.

Brokerage Firms

Although there are myriad account structures, commission plans, and marketing schemes, basically there are two types of brokerage firms:

- Discount firms, which are generally of the do-it-yourself variety.

- Full-service firms, which generally charge a commission.

Somewhere in between discount and full-service firms, there are various types of planners, advisers, and money managers. The best choice among them would be the unbiased, noncommissioned advisers who work on a flat fee or a percentage of assets basis only.

DISCOUNT BROKERS

Discount brokerage firms operate primarily with some type of flat, per-trade commission. The most prominent discount brokers include TD Waterhouse, Fidelity Brokerage, Charles Schwab, Harris Direct, Ameritrade, E-Trade, and Scottrade. These firms primarily offer investors a place to purchase their own stock selections or no-load mutual funds, although additional products and services (like those offered by the full-service firms) are becoming increasingly popular. For those investors who are willing to take some responsibility for the securities they buy, do some basic research, a little paperwork, and maintain much of their own record keeping, these top discount firms offer adequate tools. But I still think investors should adhere to long-term investing principles and utilize money managers and mutual funds because, in the long run, overly active individual investors are sure to run into trouble. Most small, active traders will buy and sell until they lose their money, just like most amateur gamblers bet until they lose everything. Unless they have the full-time research, computer models, and international buying power of a successful hedge fund, individual investors are better off investing for the long term as Warren Buffett does, rather than trying to be an active trader.

Today, some of the largest discount firms, like Schwab and Fidelity, are slowly moving into providing financial advice and money management, rather than just promoting trading activity. Investors should make sure that they find out how the person giving this advice is being compensated, so they can be sure that the advice is unbiased and in their best interest.

FEE-BASED ADVISERS

An ever-increasing number of brokers, planners, advisers, and registered representatives are getting into the fee-based business, and acting as registered investment advisers (RIA). It's a trend that I hope will continue. The basic premise is that the investor will receive unbiased advice because the adviser is only paid a flat fee or percentage for his or her recommendations and not for recommending one commissioned product over another. A truly unbiased adviser will have no problem recommending a no-load fund over a loaded fund (both of which will be explained later in this chapter).

Under an advisory agreement, and usually as part of what's called a "wrap" account, an adviser can offer fund shares that normally carry front-end sales loads, but without charging the load to the client. A wrap is simply an account where a brokerage firm helps an investor find stocks, mutual funds, or money managers in exchange for a flat quarterly or annual fee, which covers all administrative and management expenses. The management fee should be the only compensation for the adviser. No product commissions should be involved. This practice puts no-load and load funds on a level playing field.

Investors need to be leery of commissioned brokers masquerading as fee-based advisers, and need to be sure not to pay additional fees on top of commissions. Don't buy B and C shares of mutual funds (also explained in this chapter), and don't buy proprietary funds (those funds peddled by the broker's home firm).

FULL-SERVICE BROKERS

Full-service brokerages, or full-commission firms, include the major investment bank and brokerage combinations, such as Merrill Lynch, Morgan Stanley, and UBS PaineWebber; full-service, nonproprietary shops like Edward Jones and A.G. Edwards; as well as all the regional firms and independents. Most salespeople at large insurance companies like New York Life, MetLife, Northwestern, and Prudential also offer full brokerage services and are calling themselves financial planners and financial advisers.

It would take far more than a single chapter to explain all the pros and cons and possible traps of discount investing versus full-service investing. Instead, I'd like to focus on one very important point, a point that would help investors avoid a huge number of investing heartaches, and is summed up in one phrase: *Know how your broker is getting paid.* And I don't just mean knowing that they're on commission. I mean knowing exactly how they are compensated for each transaction they recommend to you. It doesn't matter if the person you're dealing with is a relative, neighbor, church member, or your kid's soccer coach—you must know how they are paid. You need to know exactly what their motivation is for recommending one particular product over another. The greater the blind level of trust, the greater the potential trap. If you know the real motivation for each recommendation, you'll be able to make a much more informed decision. The information will only help the relationship you have with your broker, not hurt it.

A FEW POTENTIAL PROBLEMS

You'd like to invest $5,000 in mutual funds and so you seek advice from a local, independent broker. The broker can sell almost any fund. For instance, an American fund has a 5.75 percent sales load (that generates the commission). The Calamos fund has a 4.75 percent load. The Fidelity fund has a 3.00 percent load. A Vanguard fund is no-load (zero commission). Which fund do you think the broker is going to recommend as the "best fund" to you, the new client?

I think they'll recommend the highest commission product first, and show you a top-ranked fund from that family.

Your cousin goes to work at a large insurance company and calls herself a financial adviser. You have an old 401(k) plan to roll over worth $23,000. Your cousin can offer numerous mutual funds with a gross commission of 4 percent to 5 percent, but she also has a variable annuity product that pays a 5 percent commission. The annuity also helps meet her required three-month sales quota since it's a company product. As a new agent, the company product also qualifies for a 50 percent bonus on top of commissions at the end of the month. Even with the best intentions, what product do you think your cousin will recommend first?

You should expect to receive a convincing sales presentation on the benefits of the high-commission annuity.

You have an account at a large, well-known, national broker. You have an interest in aggressive investments. XYZ, Inc., a tech stock, has been in the news and seems to have good growth prospects, so you mention it to your broker. You don't know that the stock is not "covered" by his firm's research analysts. Instead, the broker recommends ABC Technology Company and shows you that his firm rates it a "strong buy." The broker's firm's investment banking arm is also underwriting a new $100 million bond offering of ABC Tech. Can you see any conflict of interest? Do you think that the broker will be compensated any differently by selling ABC, rather than XYZ? Will the broker be recognized and supported by his firm any differently for selling ABC? Do you trust the "strong buy" recommendation?

The broker wants and needs to sell the ABC Technology stock. I think the "strong buy" recommendation is obviously worthless.

Mutual Funds

Mutual funds are simply a compilation of stocks, bonds, or other individual securities determined by a fund manager, with many investors pooling their money together in a joint investment. The individual investments of each fund are dependent upon the overall objective of the fund. When these investments rise or fall in value, you gain or lose with them. Most mutual funds are called open-end, which means that new shares are continuously issued as more investors choose to buy them. Shares of mutual funds can usually be redeemed at the close of any business day.

In the world of mutual funds, you generally have two choices: No-load funds or loaded (commissioned) funds. I work with no-load funds. There are no commissions, and therefore no salesperson to try to sell you the fund from a biased point of view.

I believe you should always buy funds no-load. You can either deal directly with a no-load fund company or buy no-load funds through a discount brokerage firm. If you want investment advice or money management, you can deal with a fee-based, unbiased adviser who can work with loaded mutual funds on a no-load basis.

NO-LOAD FUNDS

No-load means no commission. There's no sales charge on the front end or the back end. Investors either need to make their own investment decisions—basically self-service—or buy funds through a fee-based adviser. Of course, no-load fund companies are not charity organizations. All mutual funds have management and other fees that make up the total expense ratio—obviously the lower, the better. Many funds are able to, or at least should be able to, decrease their total expanse ratios over long periods of time after their overall assets grow. Many no-load funds are beginning to add short-term redemption fees. They usually are 1 percent to 2 percent of the sum redeemed and apply only to redemptions within thirty days to six months of purchase. These costs should not be confused with back-end surrender charges that are imposed on loaded mutual funds. These new, short-term redemption fees are there only to help protect the fund and its shareholders from short term, market-timing traders.

LOADED FUNDS

With a loaded fund, someone is probably making a commission. Today, the commissioned mutual fund arena has turned into an alphabet soup of various expense and commission structures. A shares, B shares, and C shares are the most common.

Some fund companies are adding share classes D, F, T, Y, and others. If you see one of these letters, or share classes, you're probably buying a loaded mutual fund. Although this seems like a relatively simple concept, I want to spell it out because I'm constantly amazed by the number of people who have purchased loaded mutual funds without knowing that they're paying a commission.

Brokers are required to explain the various share class options each time they make a recommendation or sale. Unfortunately, they very rarely do. Most brokers sell whatever share class is easiest to sell, or whatever their favorite is. Either way, they're making a commission. B shares and C shares, with back-end surrender charges instead of front-end loads, are all too often presented to perspective investors as no-load funds. They aren't. In addition to having surrender penalties, these B and C shares usually carry greatly inflated internal expenses to help cover the commissions that are still going to the broker. B shares and C shares are often the most expensive way to buy a fund in the long run.

With all the various expense structures associated with loaded funds, comparing funds side by side can be difficult. Most fund-performance graphs and yearly data do not take sales charges (especially back-end or deferred sales charges) into account even though the front-end or back-end loads can severely cut into fund performance.

There is, however, some good news in dealing with loaded funds. It's a little known fact, but regular, front-loaded A shares of most funds can usually be purchased without the load. Very few investors understand that loaded funds can be purchased this way, and very few brokers will ever be willing to explain how it can be done. In the prospectus of most loaded mutual funds (the prospectus that many investors unfortunately don't read), right under the section usually called "How to Purchase Shares," there is usually an explanation of all the methods to purchase a fund without the load. Brokers can usually waive the sales load if they have you sign an investment advisory agreement, or purchase your funds inside the wrap account that I mentioned earlier. Wrap accounts are available to almost all modern brokers.

Advice for Investors

By now, it should be obvious to readers that I am a proponent of long-term investing with a disciplined, slow-trading strategy. In his Berkshire Hathaway 1990 annual report, Warren Buffett stated, "Lethargy bordering on sloth remains the cornerstone of our investment style." Although he's exaggerating somewhat—his annual reports are often hilarious—I couldn't agree more. As stated earlier in the book, investors should buy great companies and own them for long periods of time.

In this chapter, I've also written a great deal about fees. Although low fees are important, simply avoiding fees is not nearly as important as understanding fees. Mutual funds and brokerage accounts have fees. It's a necessary part of doing business. Investors need to understand fee structures so they can properly weigh the trade-offs between fees, performance, and service.

Here is a checklist of advice for investors.

- Invest for the long term. Don't be swayed by books, seminars, or infomercials about options, futures, or day trading. Buy good companies or funds, hold them for the long term, and invest like great investors Warren Buffett and Peter Lynch.

- Don't listen to the press. Don't invest with the herd. Warren Buffett had referred to the investing public as "lemmings."

Don't be one of them. Much of the market's short-term actions are caused by the herd mentality of average investors. The financial press amplifies the problem, causing investors to buy and sell much too often and usually at the wrong times. In the spring of 2000, while the market was at a peak, stock mutual funds were receiving new investor dollars at a record pace. Fund outflows are usually highest when the market is at a low.

- Use short-term fluctuations as buying opportunities. Short-term stock price changes create opportunities for long-term investors. Negative press, short-term earnings reports, legal proceedings (depending on severity), and regulatory problems cause stock prices to dip when the investing public overreacts. Remember to buy low and sell high. Over time, stock prices will usually follow a solid company's long-term earnings and should bounce back from price dips.

- Diversify your investments. Spreading your investments over various industries, sectors, and investment styles is extremely important. I own growth stocks and value stocks, large cap stocks and small cap stocks, and stocks spread over at least four industries. I honestly have no idea whether alcohol, gaming, tobacco, or defense will lead the way in any given month or year.

- Rebalance your portfolio regularly. A diversified portfolio will grow out of balance with time. You'll end up owning more of the past years' top-performing area and less of the underperforming area. Human nature causes average investors to buy more of the "hot" stocks and sell the losers. Do the opposite. Sell some of the top performers—sell high. Buy more of the underperformers—buy low. As long as you own strong stocks in solid industries, odds are that your underperformers will bounce back, and last year's top performers will lag.

- Dollar-cost average. Dollar-cost averaging means adding a set amount of money to an account on a regular basis, usually monthly. When the market dips, your fixed monthly investment buys more shares. When the market is high, you buy fewer shares. Adding money on a regular basis doesn't guarantee results, but it is an automatic way to help you buy shares at lower average prices, and build an investment account over time.

- Buy no-load mutual funds. With thousands of mutual funds available, buy only funds on a no-load basis. There's no need to be hit with front-end sales charges or back-end surrender penalties. While there are some very, very good loaded funds available, there's almost always a comparable no-load fund that could be picked instead. The funds may be virtually the same except for the sales load.

- Use discount brokerage firms. Discount brokerage firms are just that, discount. Their fees are straightforward and simple. They offer all types of stock brokerage accounts, mutual funds, and cash management services—as long as you're willing to do some level of self-service. If you have a full-service, major brokerage firm account and think you aren't paying a great deal more for it, you're mistaken and don't truly understand how the broker is getting compensated.

- Use unbiased, fee-based advisers. If you need or want one-on-one investment advice, use an unbiased, fee-based adviser. Thankfully, more and more brokers are offering fee-based advice and money management. There's nothing wrong with seeking advice. In fact, I strongly recommend it. Fee-based advisers are only paid for their time, or for the amount of money managed. They are not compensated differently for selling one product over another, and are therefore unbiased—not commission driven.

I believe that if you follow the advice of *Investing in Vice*, despite the inevitable ups and downs of the stock market, you can create a portfolio likely to be recession-proof for years to come.

Index

Index

Index

Index

Index

Index

Index

Index

Index

Index

Index